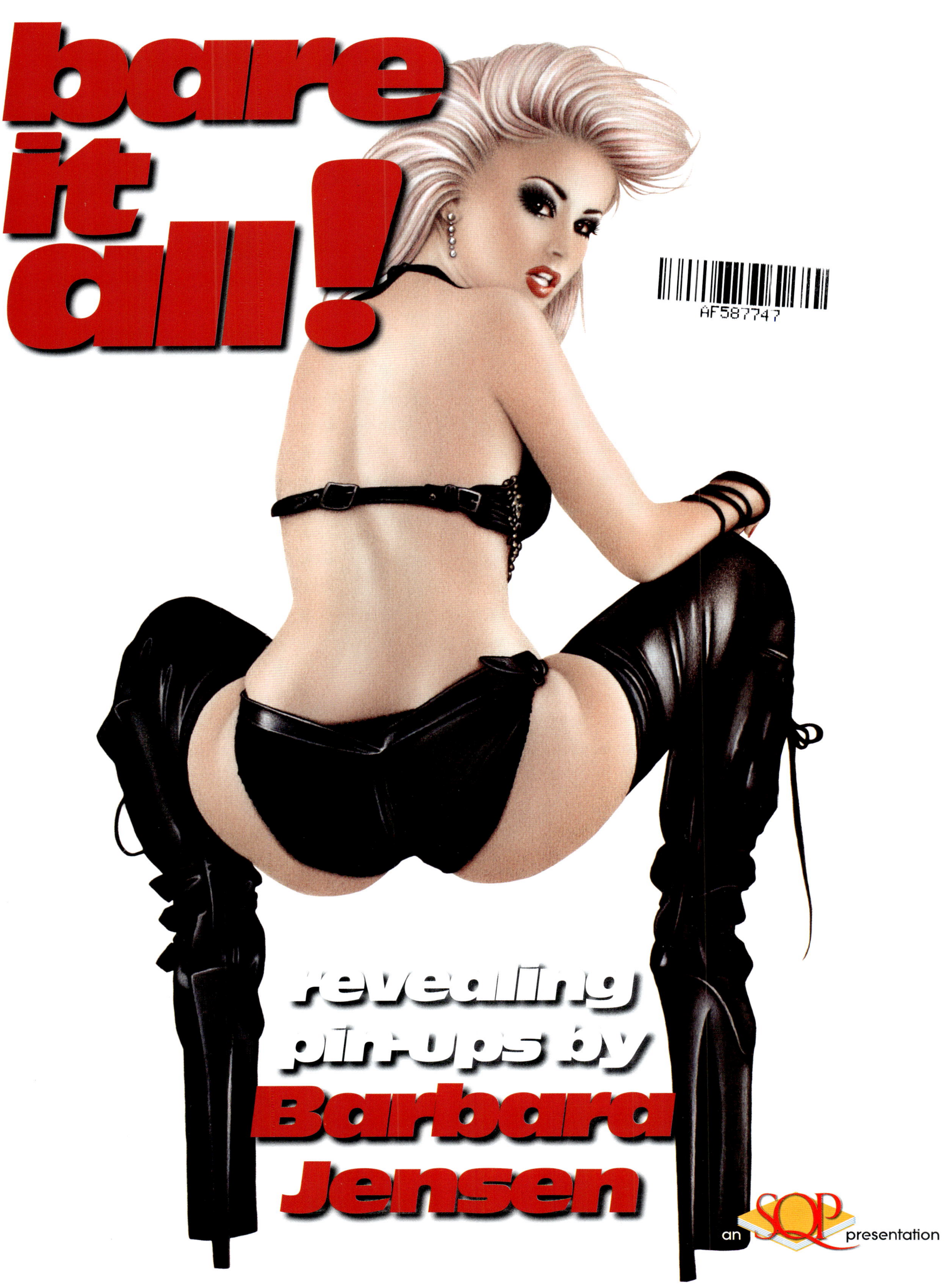
bare
it
all!
AF587747
revealing
pin-ups by
Barbara
Jensen
an SQP presentation

Bare It All!

Revealing Pin-Ups by

Barbara Jensen

I would like to thank all of the models and photographers who have trusted me with their work

Models:
Bianca Beauchamp (www.biancabeauchamp.com)
Miss Mosh (www.themoshroom.com)
Kayden Kross (www.clubkayden.com)
Michelle Thorne (www.michellethorne.com)
Ulorin Vex (www.ulorinvex.com)
Leila Lewis (www.theleilalewis.com)
Razor Candi (www.razorcandi.com)
Rubberdoll (www.rubberdoll.net)
SINderella Rockafella
(www.facebook.com/SINderellaRockafellePinUp/timeline)
Romanie (www.facebook.com/romaniesmithmodel)
Aria Giovanni

Photographers:
Suze Randall (www.suze.net)
Holly Randall (www.hollyrandall.com)
Dan Richards (http://d2L2.deviantart.com)
Martin Perreault (www.marticperreault.com)
Juliland (www.juiland.com)
Bolo Janos Attila

Prints and galleries of Barbara's work can be found at
www.Eroticartistgallery.com

For psp graphic afficiandos, her tubes can be found at
www.Barbarajensentubes.com

For the legion of Etsy shoppers, there's now
www.etsy.com/shop/Arteest111

Would you like to commission your very own piece of original Barbara Jensen art?
Contact her directly at
Arteest111@aol.com

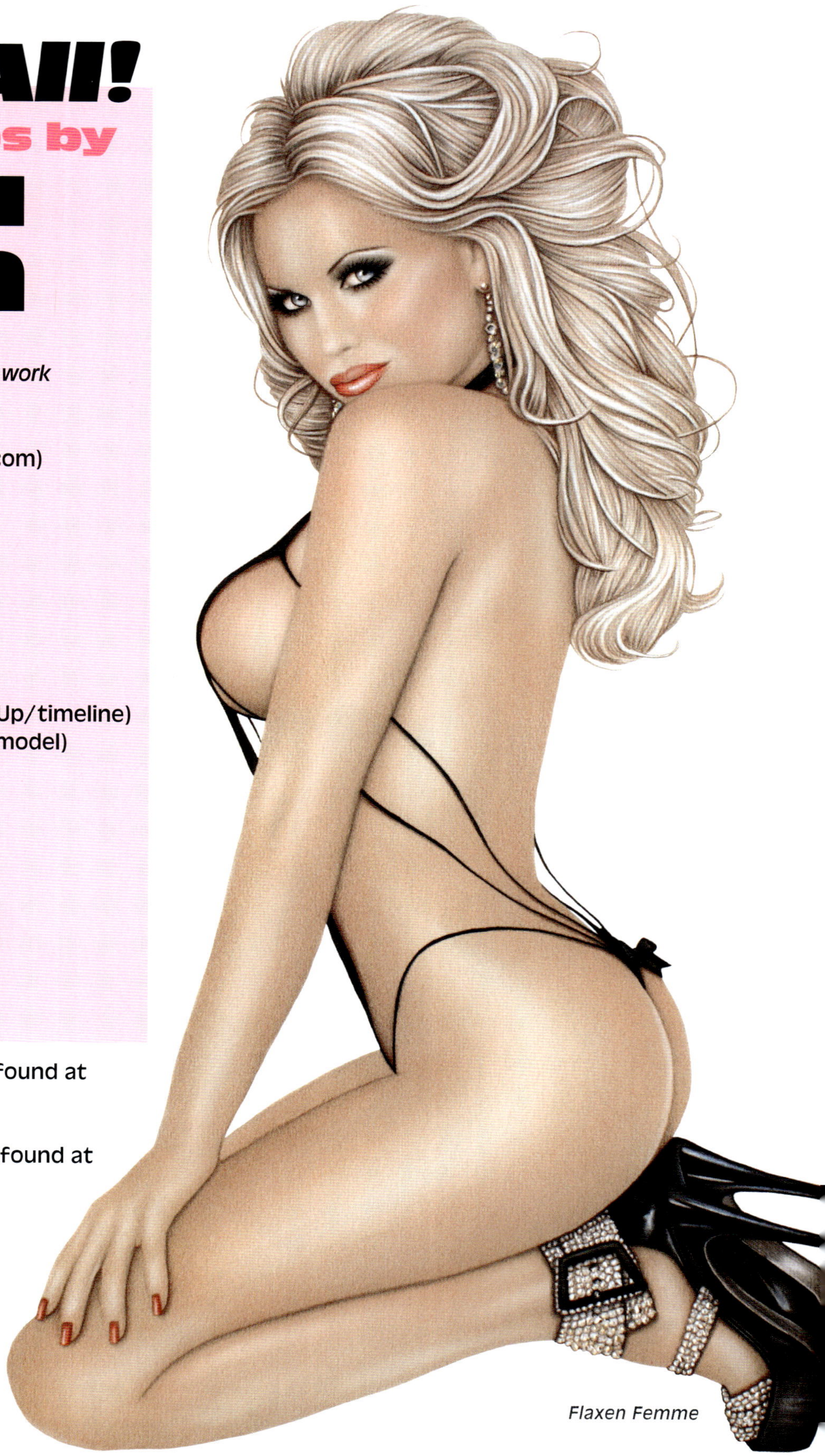

Flaxen Femme

Bare It All! Revealing Pin-Ups by Barbara Jensen

Book design by Grassy Knoll Studios.

Published by SQP Inc. - PO Box 248 - Columbus NJ 08022

Sal Quartuccio & Bob Keenan - Publishers

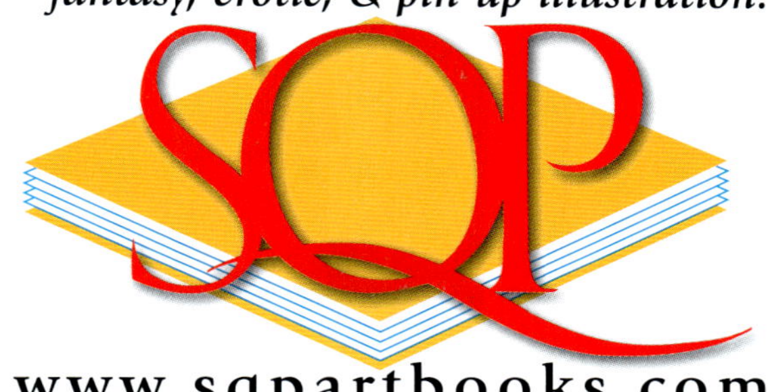

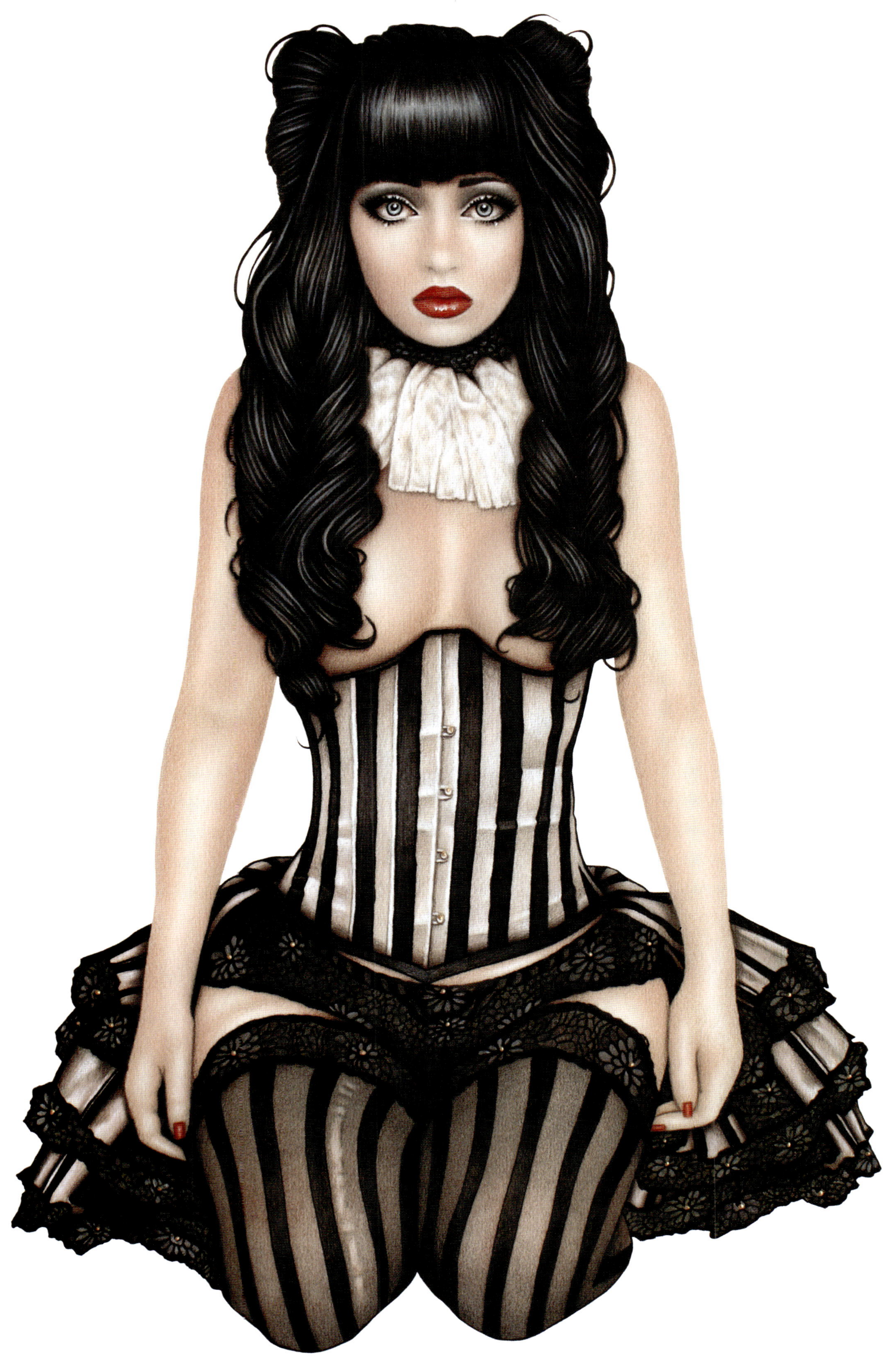

Sad Sack

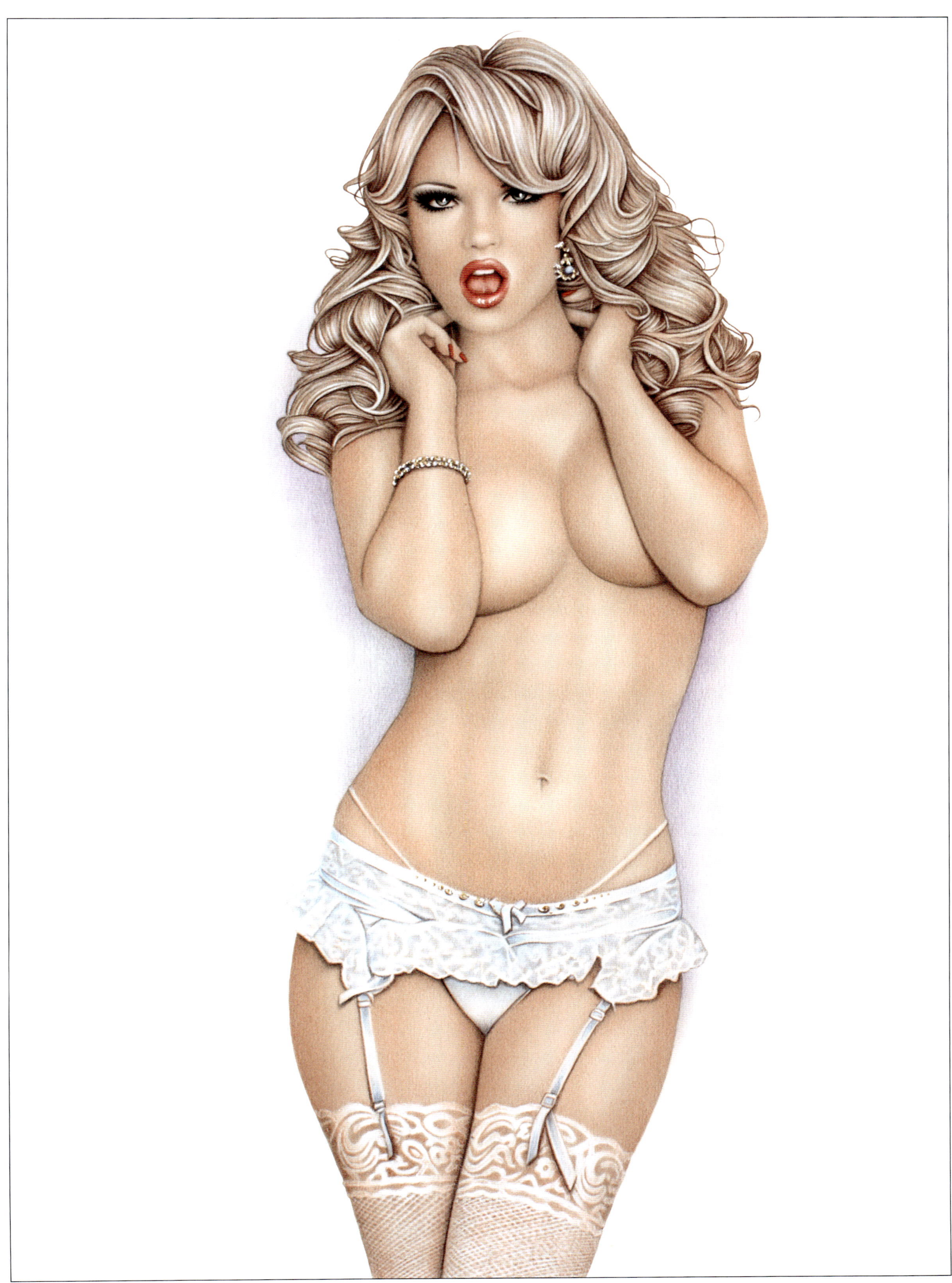

Surprise Party

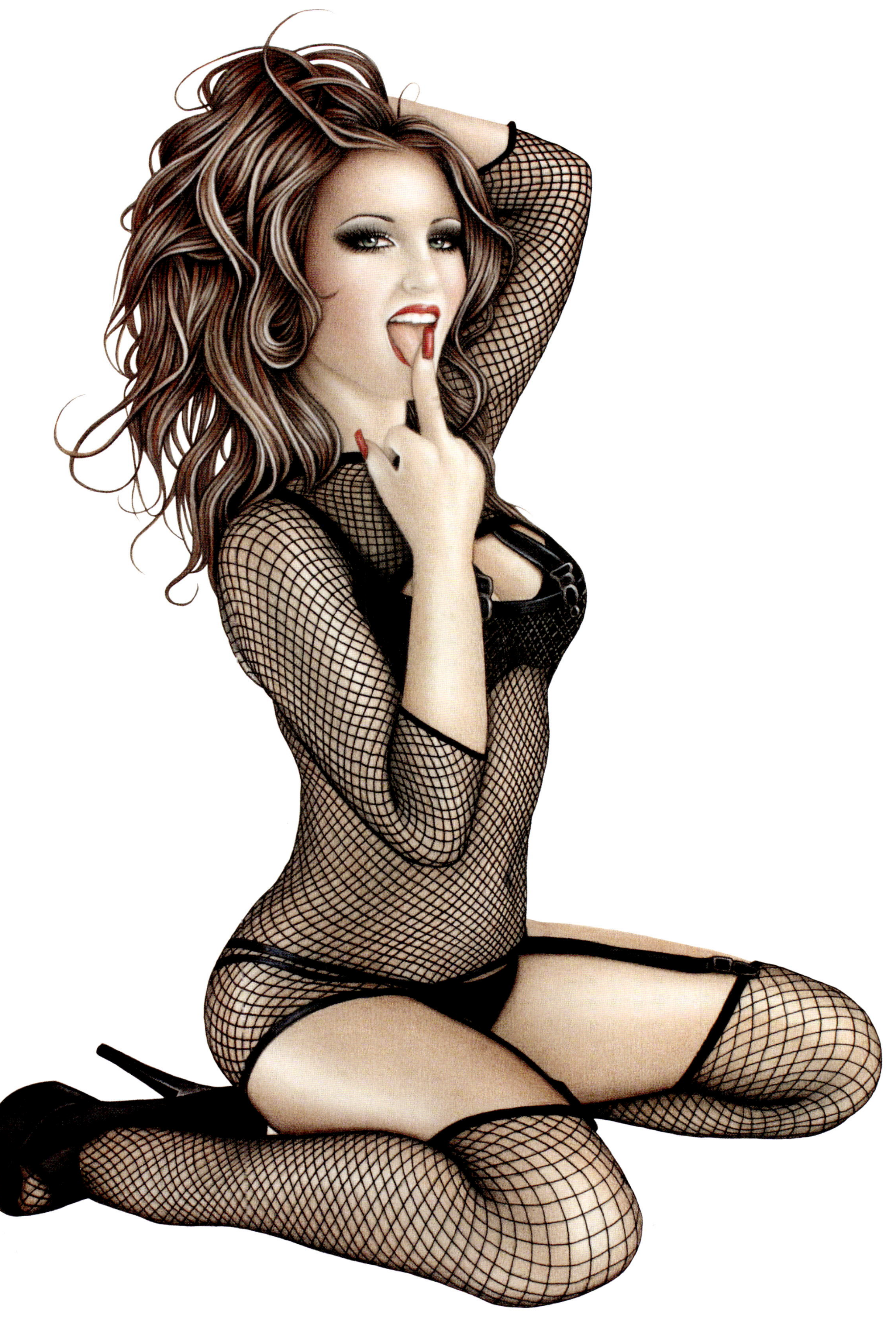

Devour

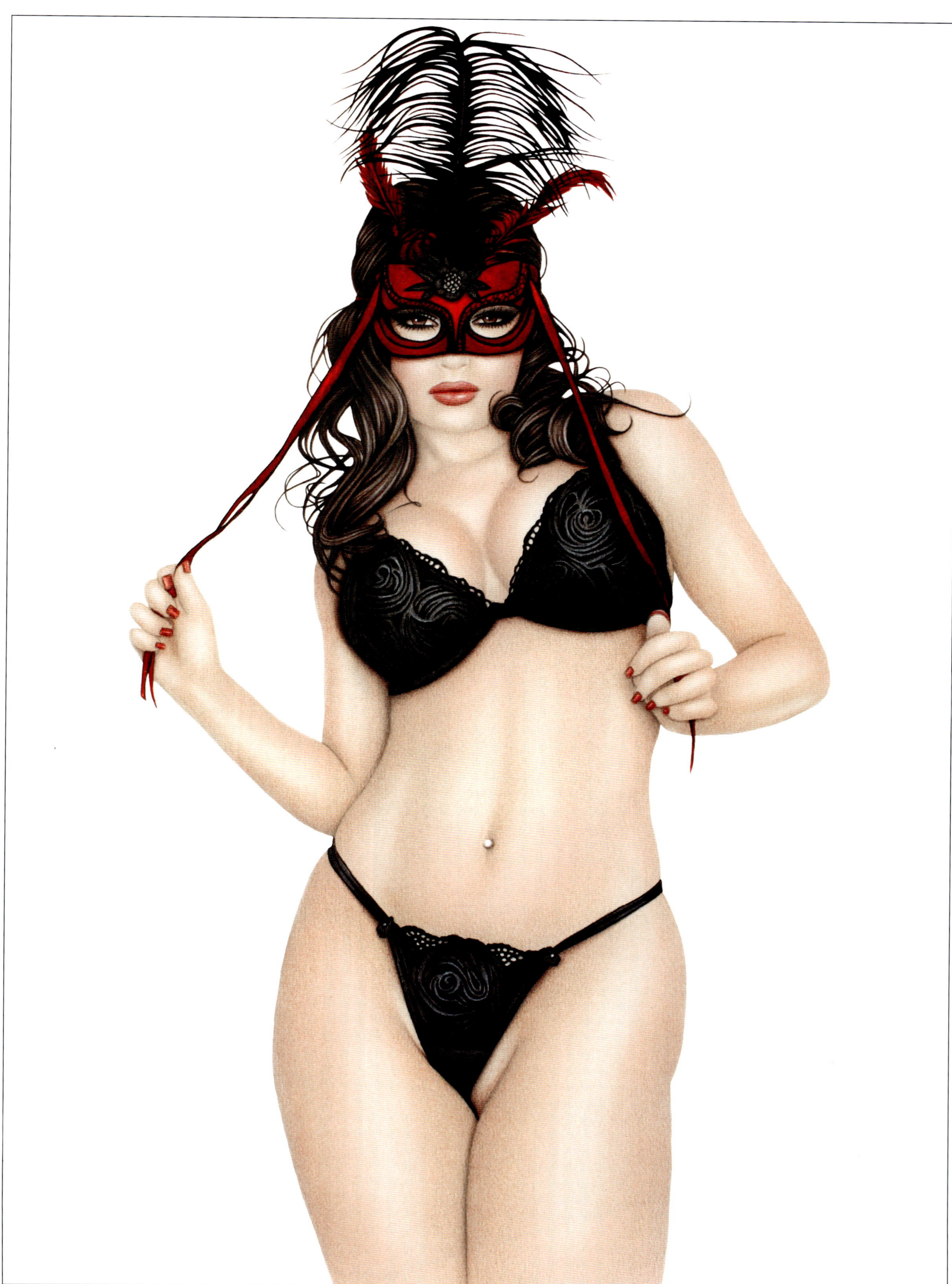

Masquerade

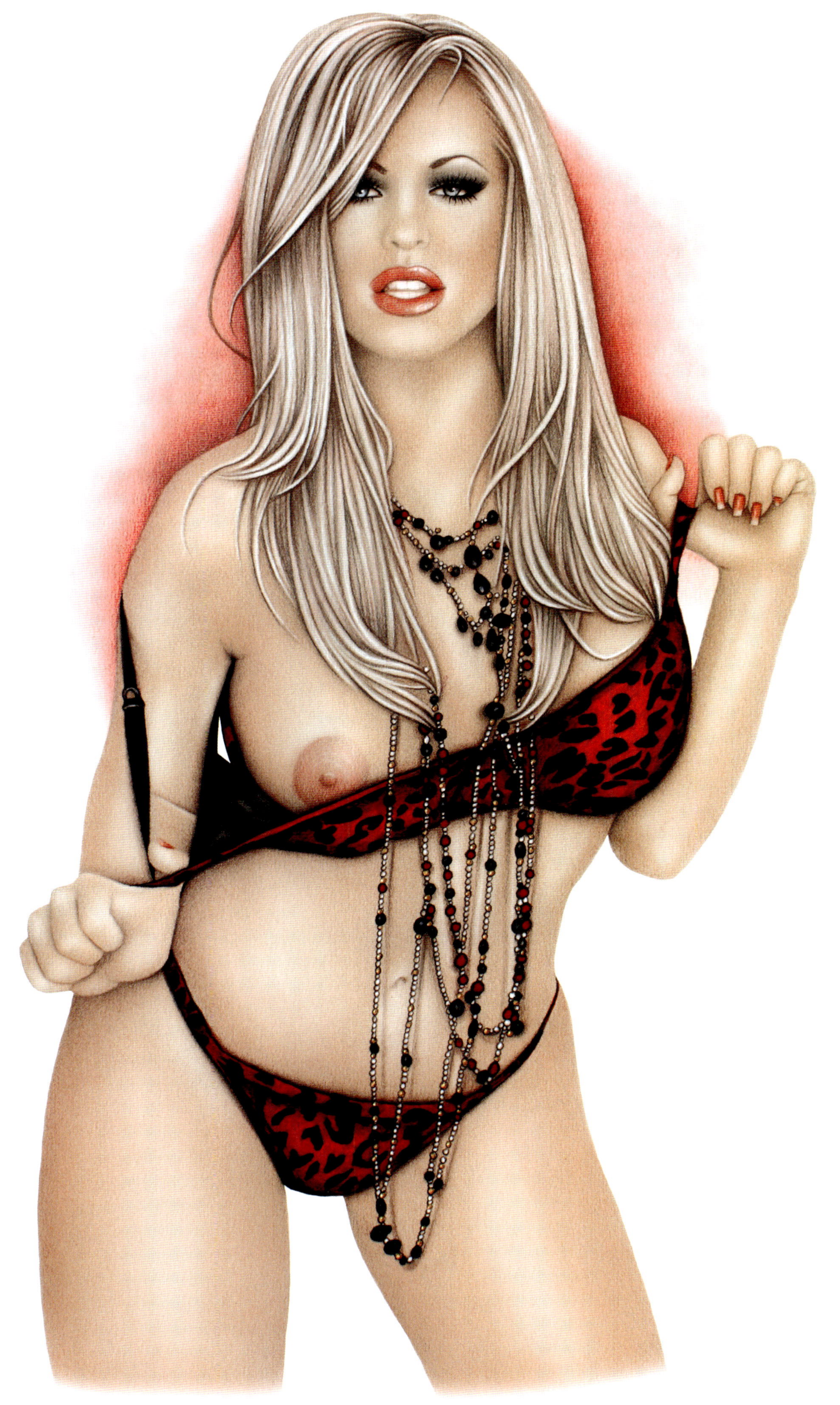

Red Leopard

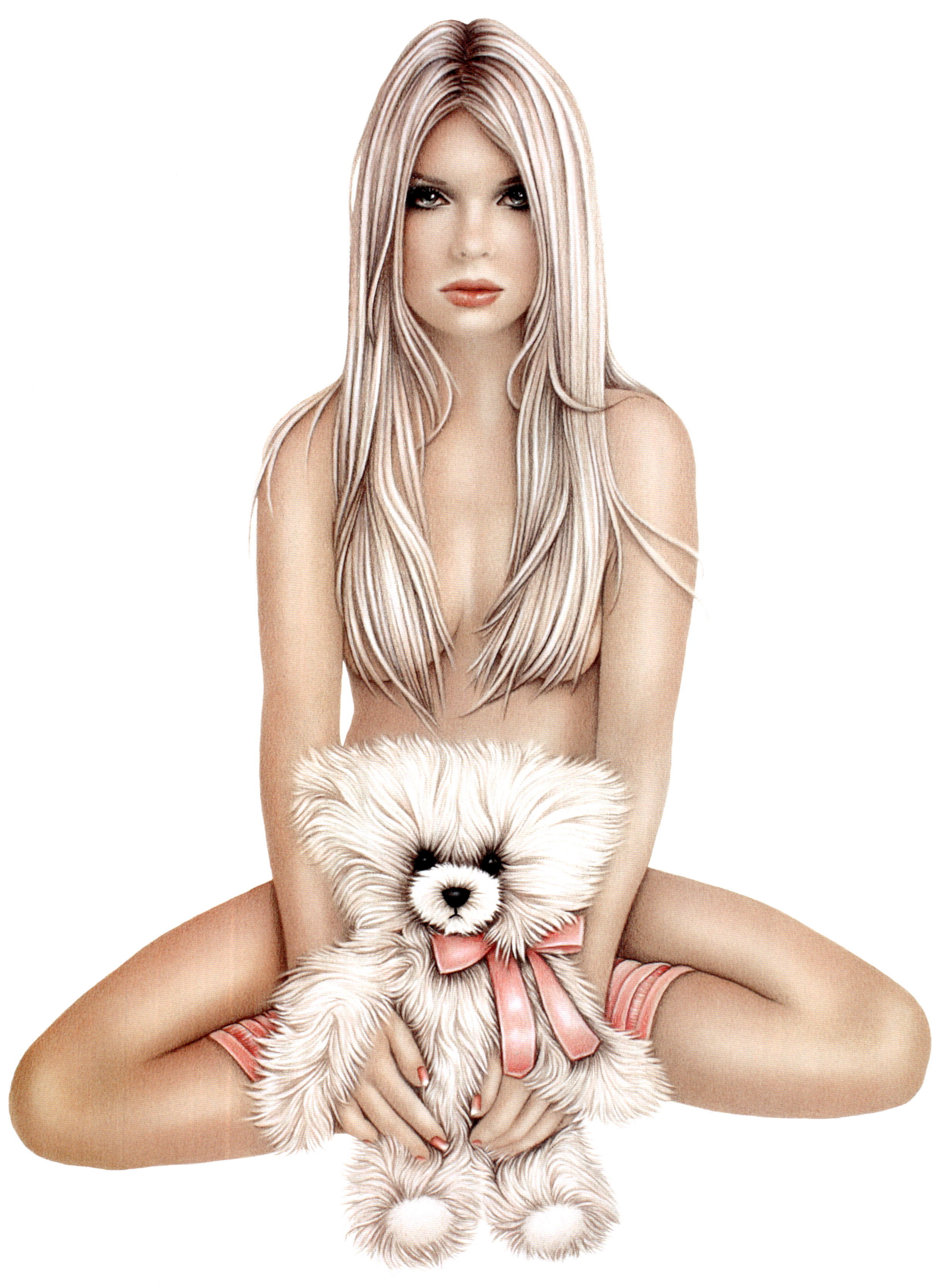

Teddy Bare

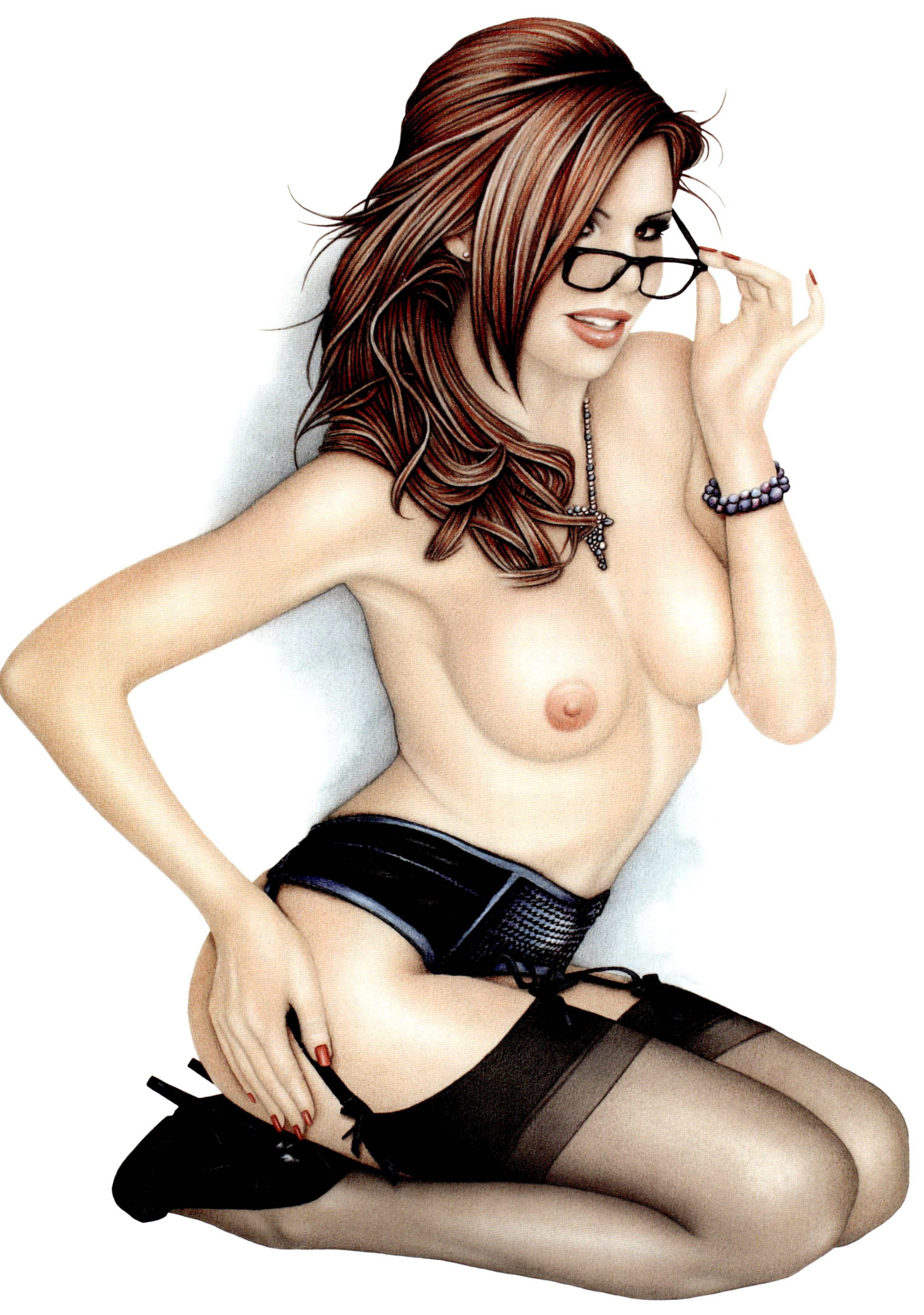

My New Specs

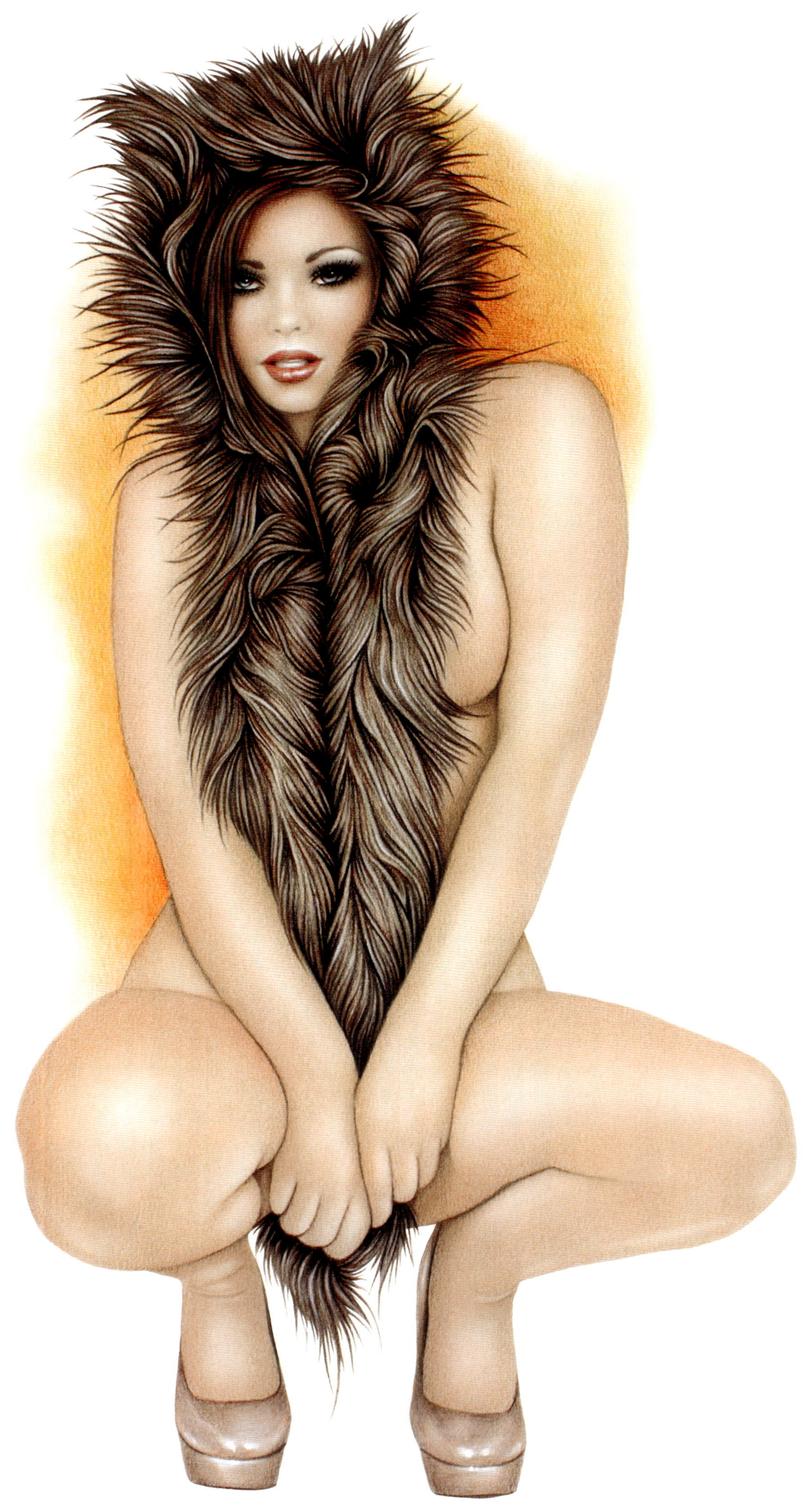

Foxy

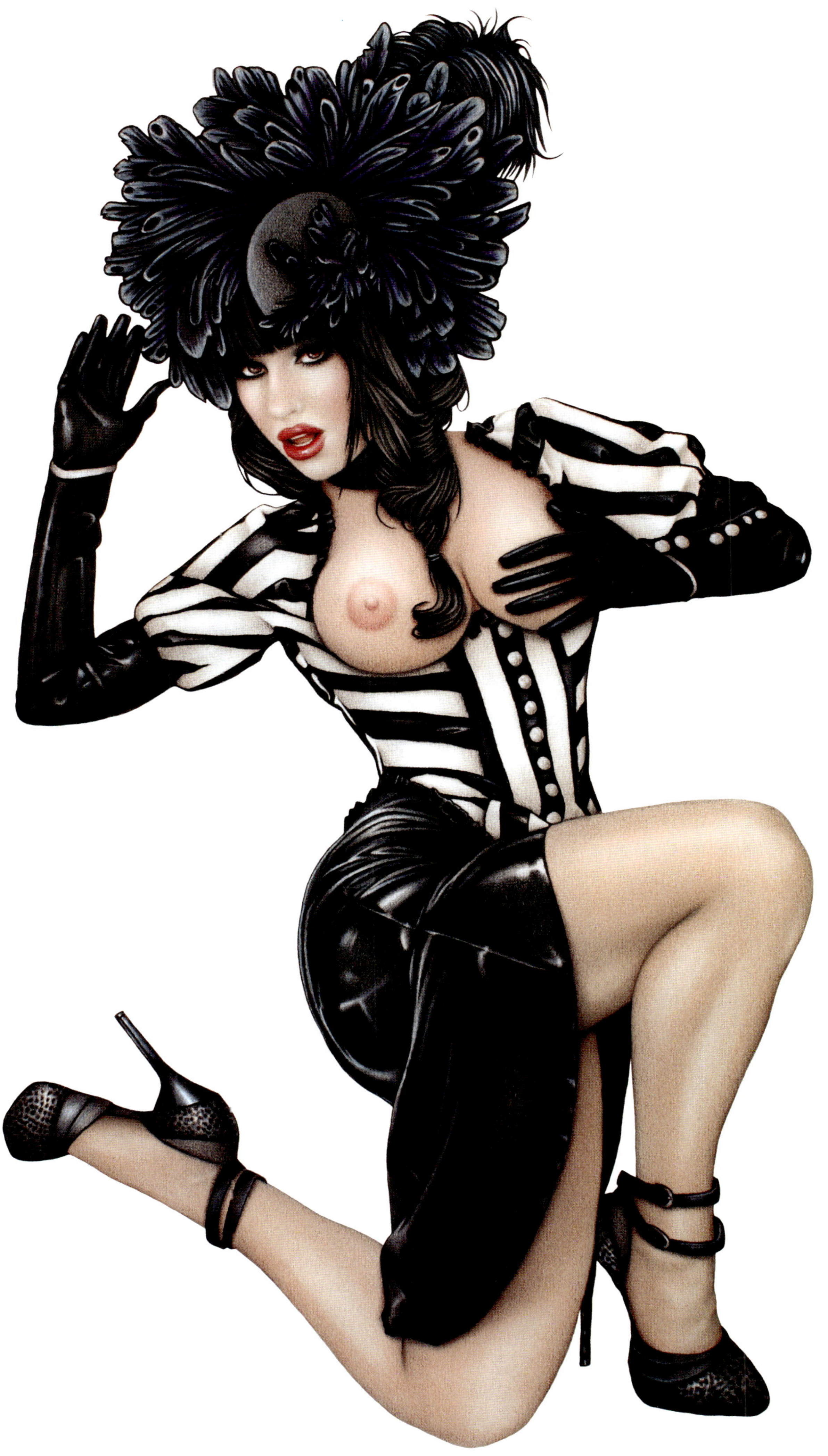

Fine Feathered

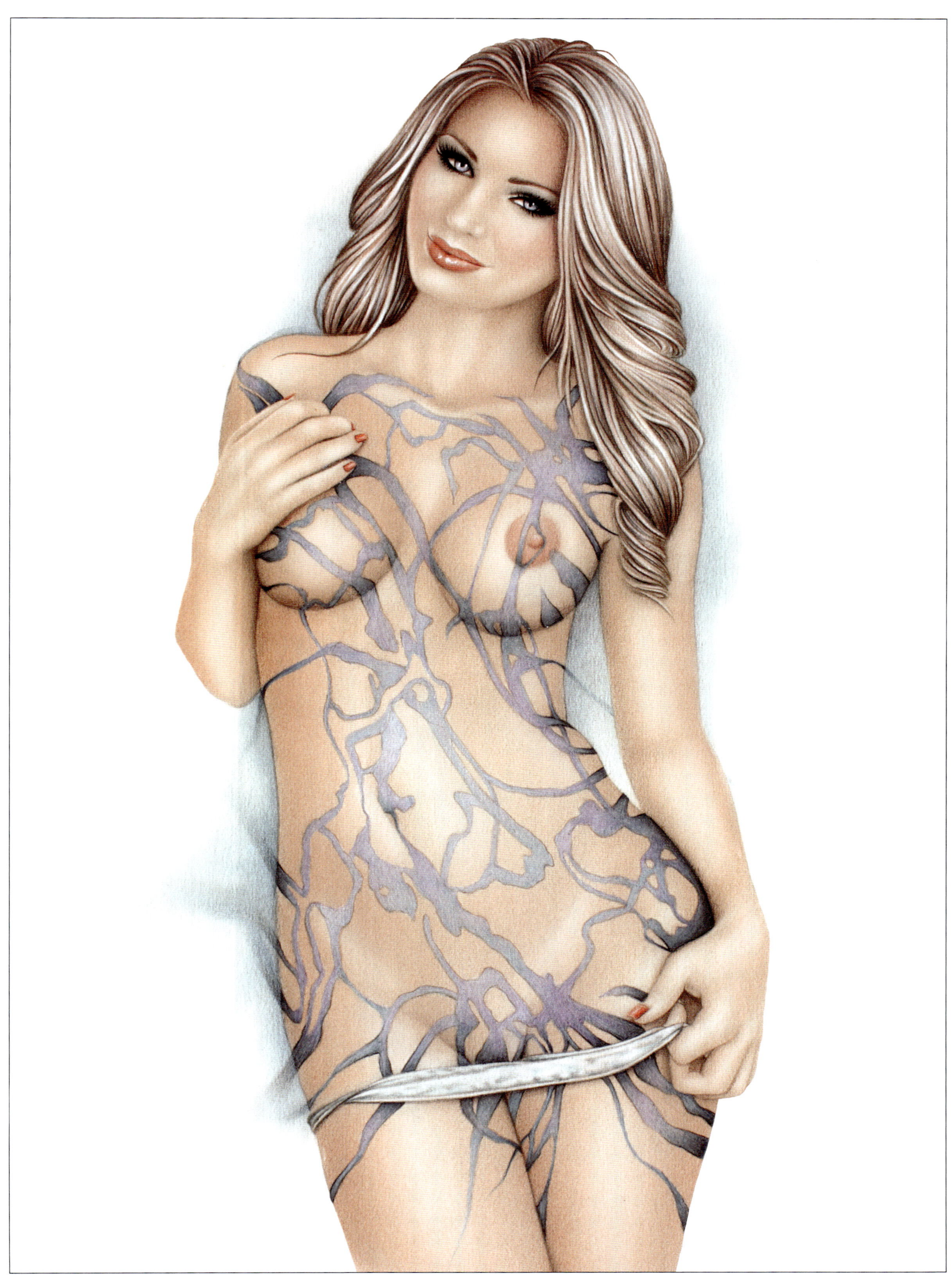

Aqua Marine

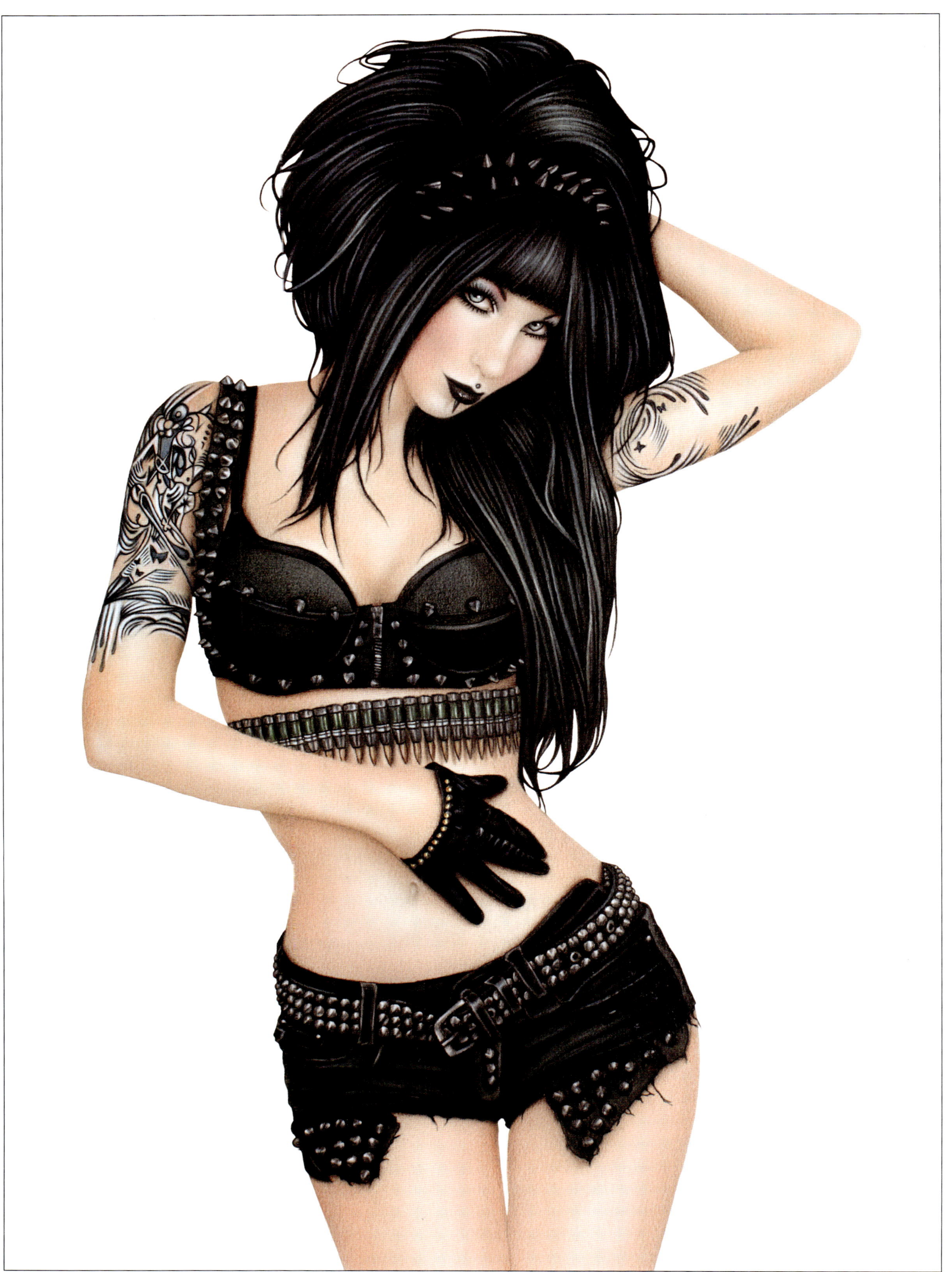

Cutting Edge

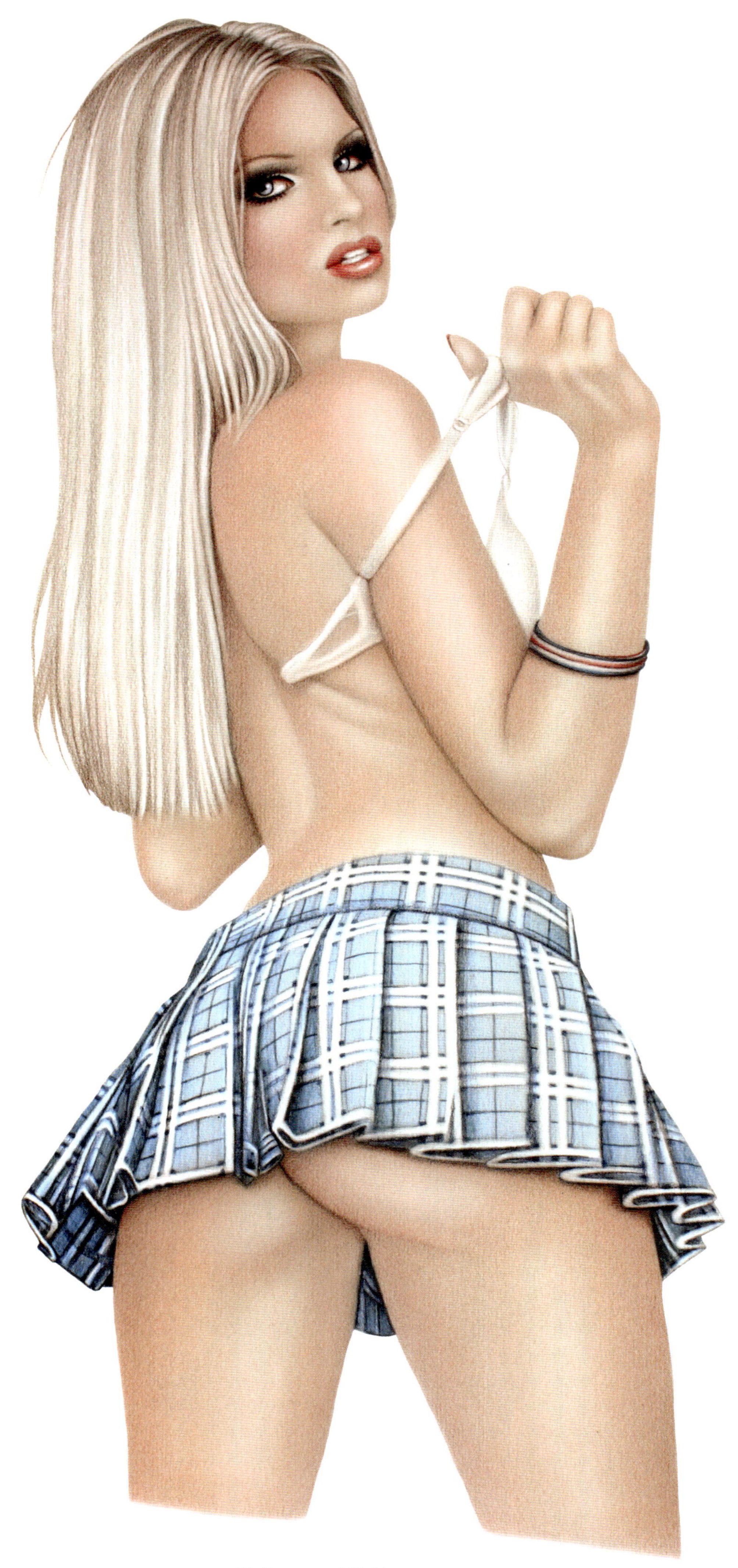

Platinum and Plaid

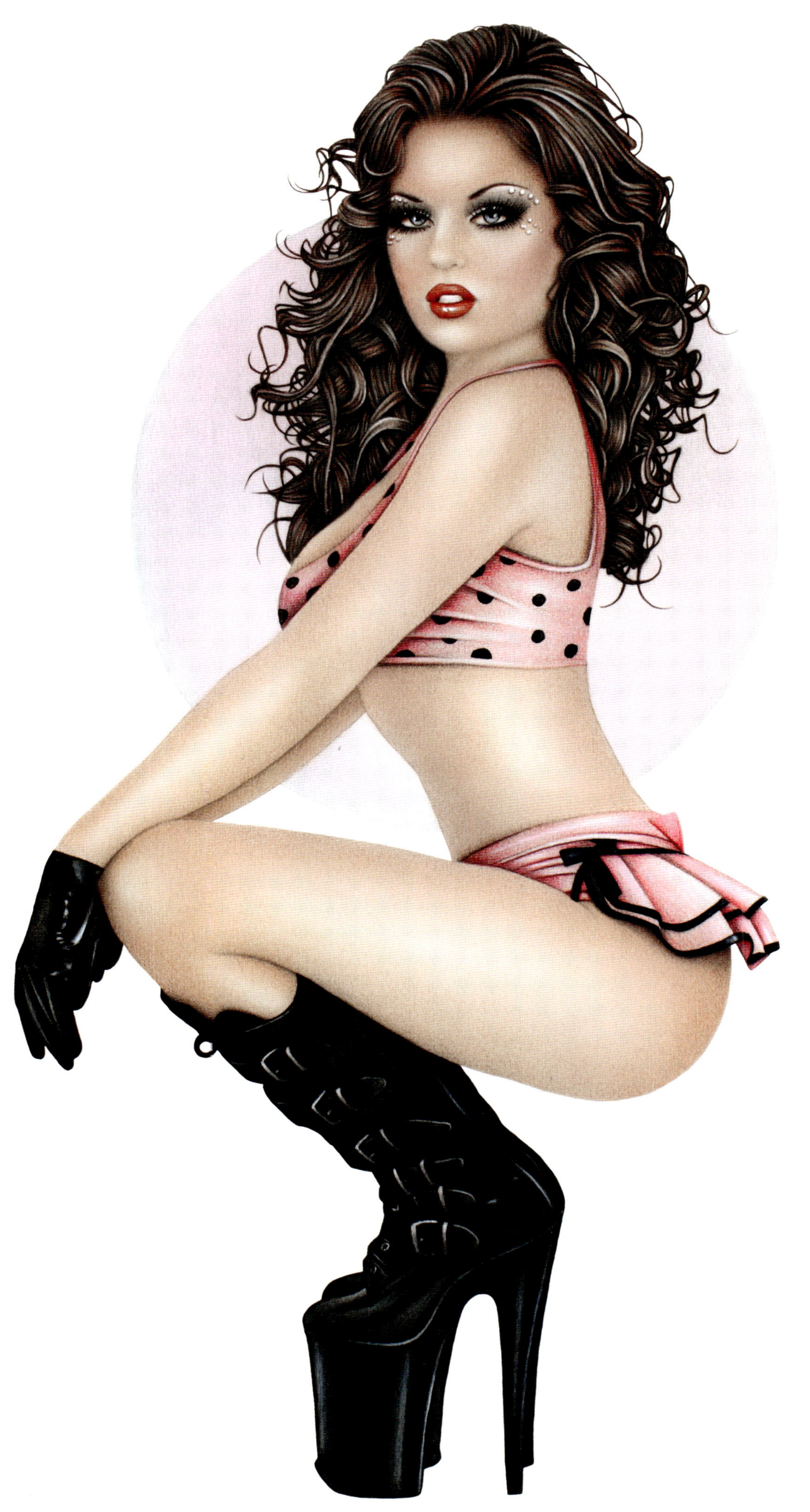

Moon Child

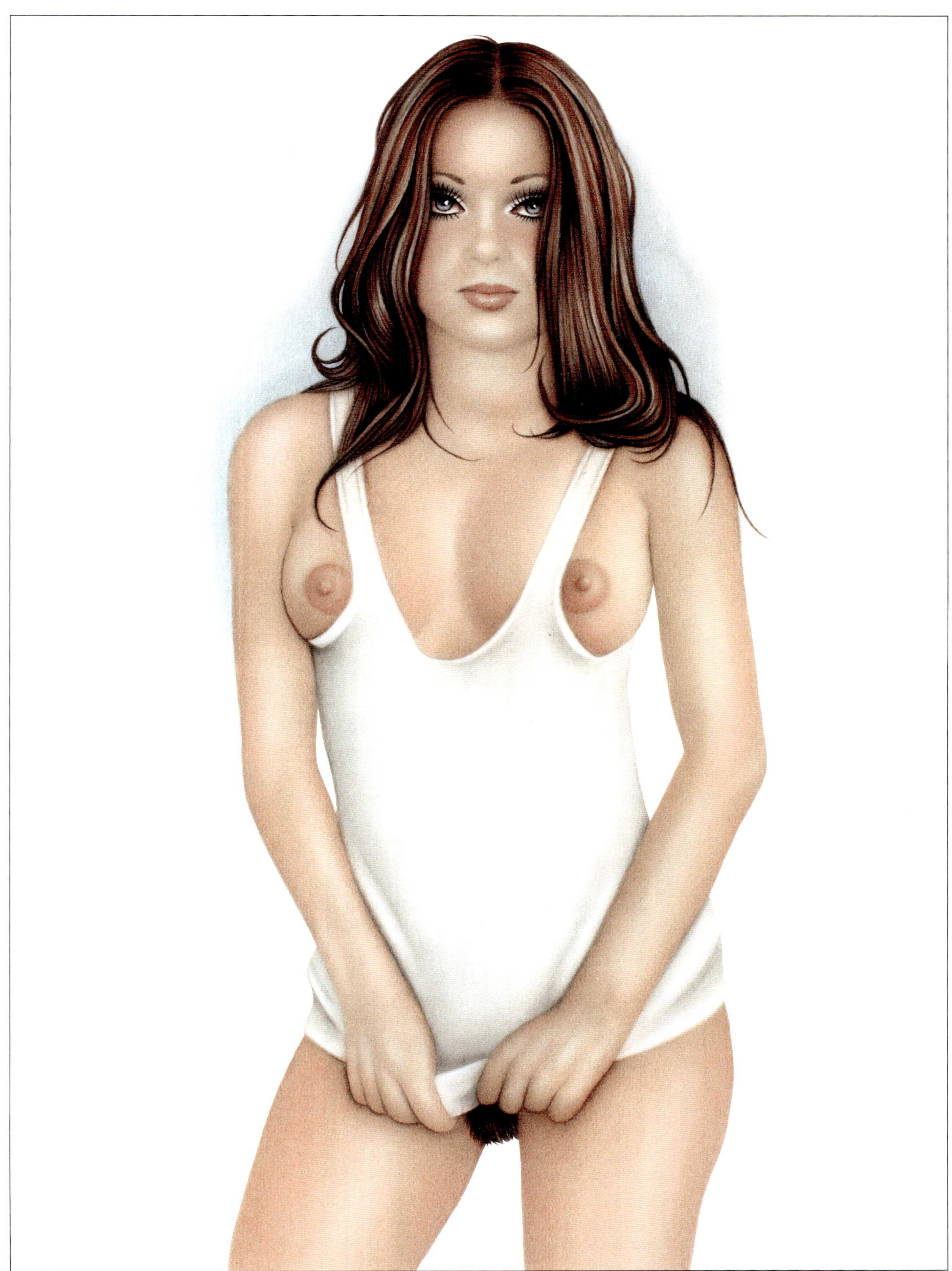

Nameless

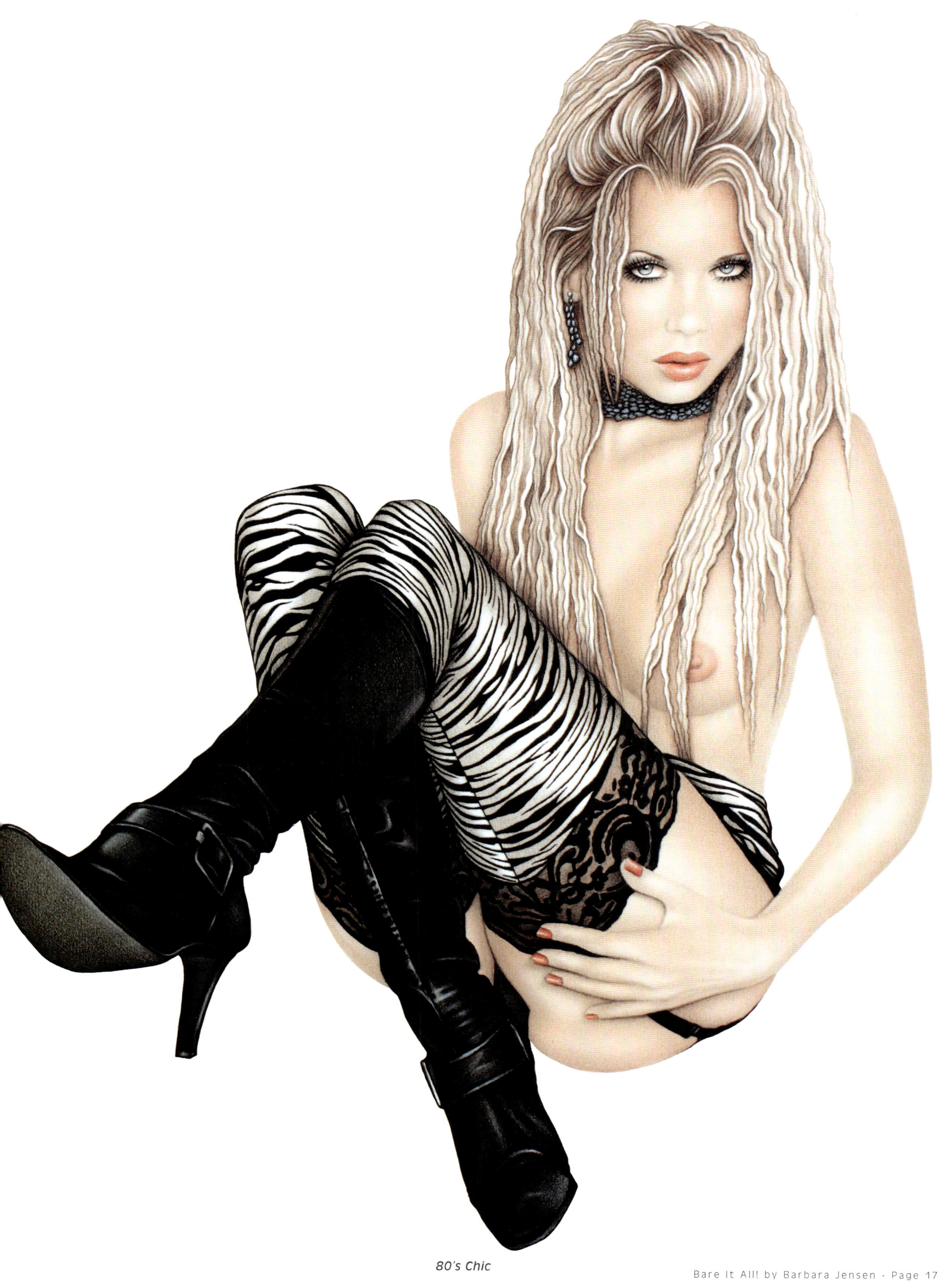

80's Chic

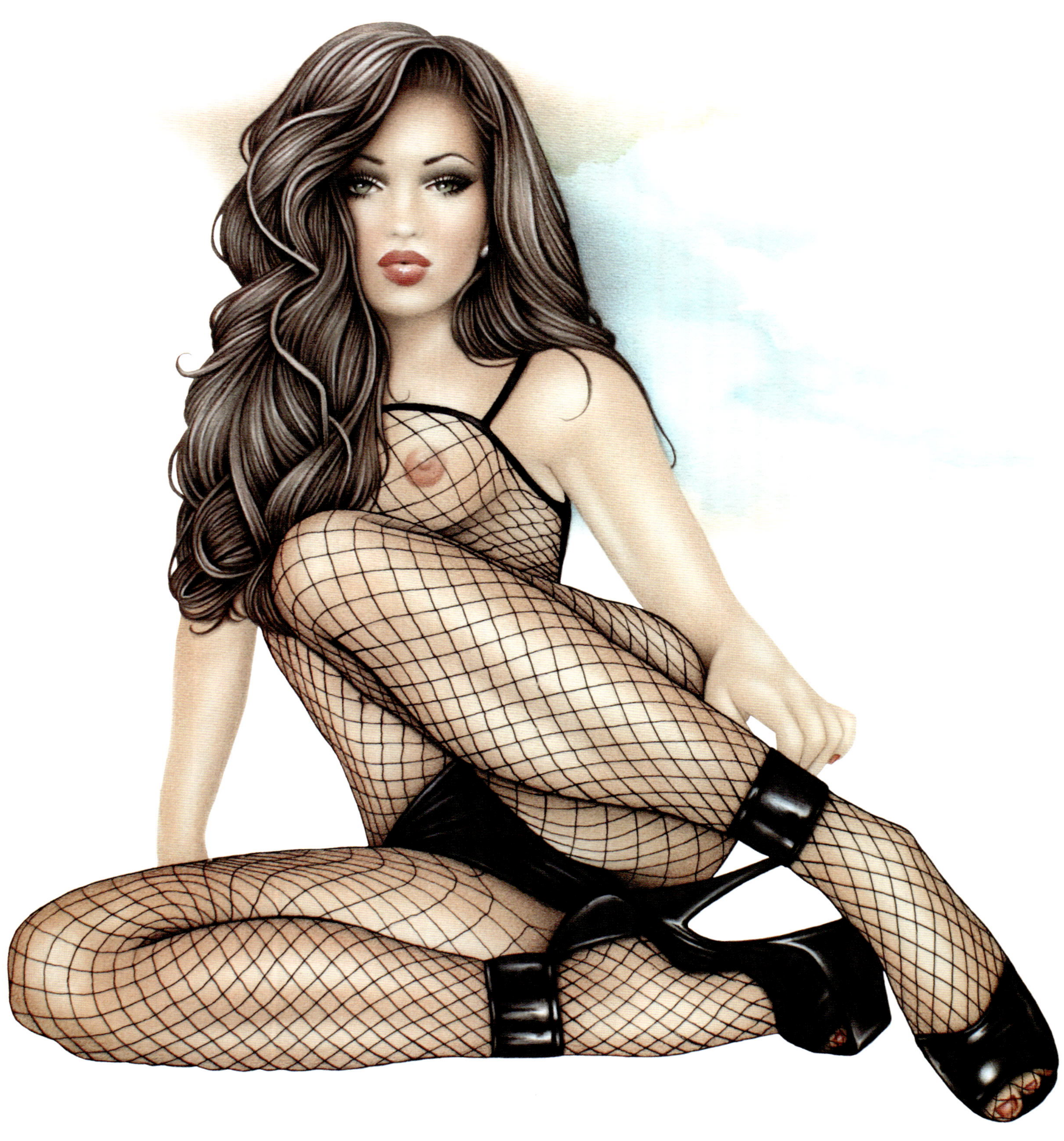

Lolita

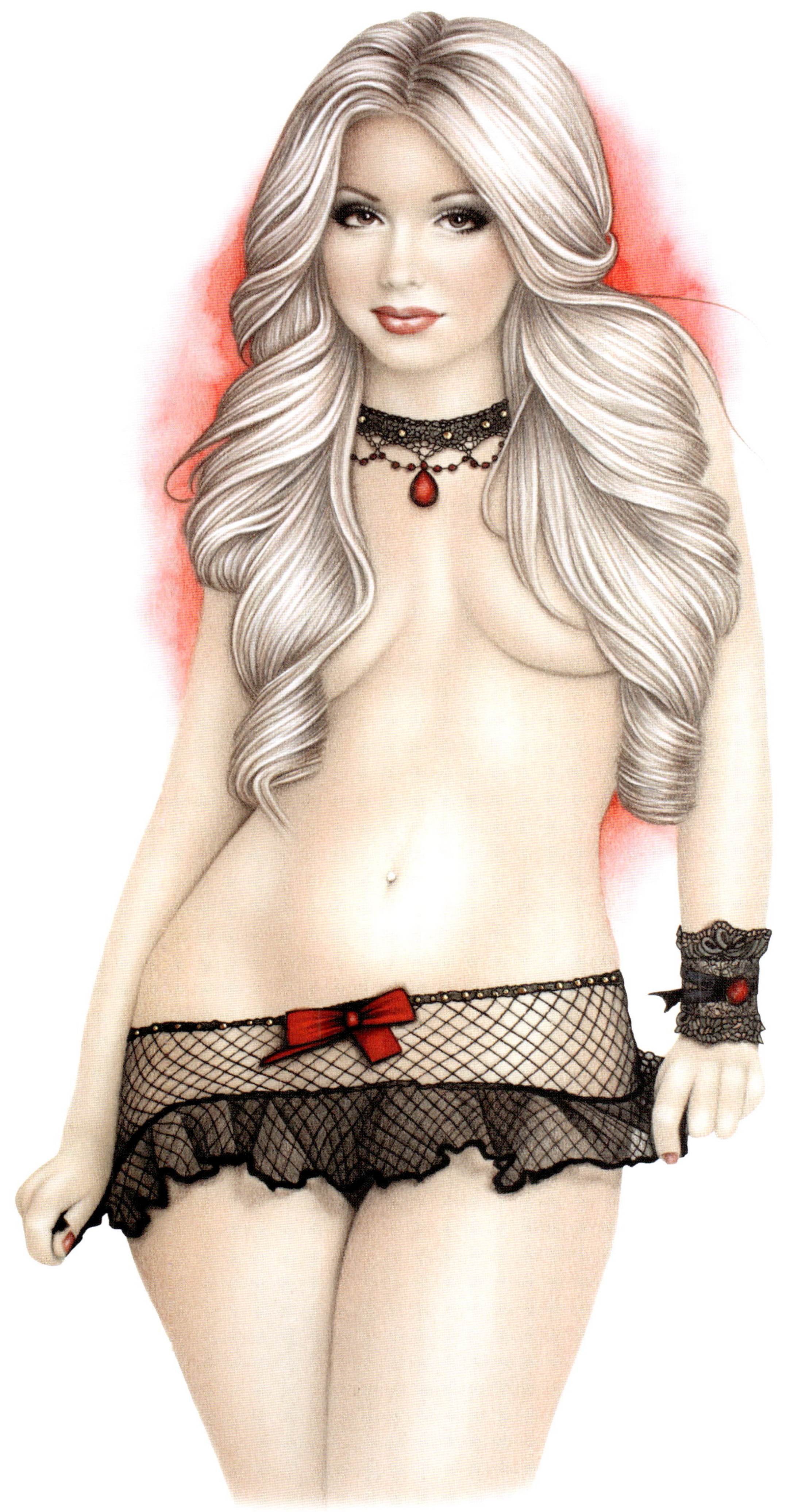

Carmine

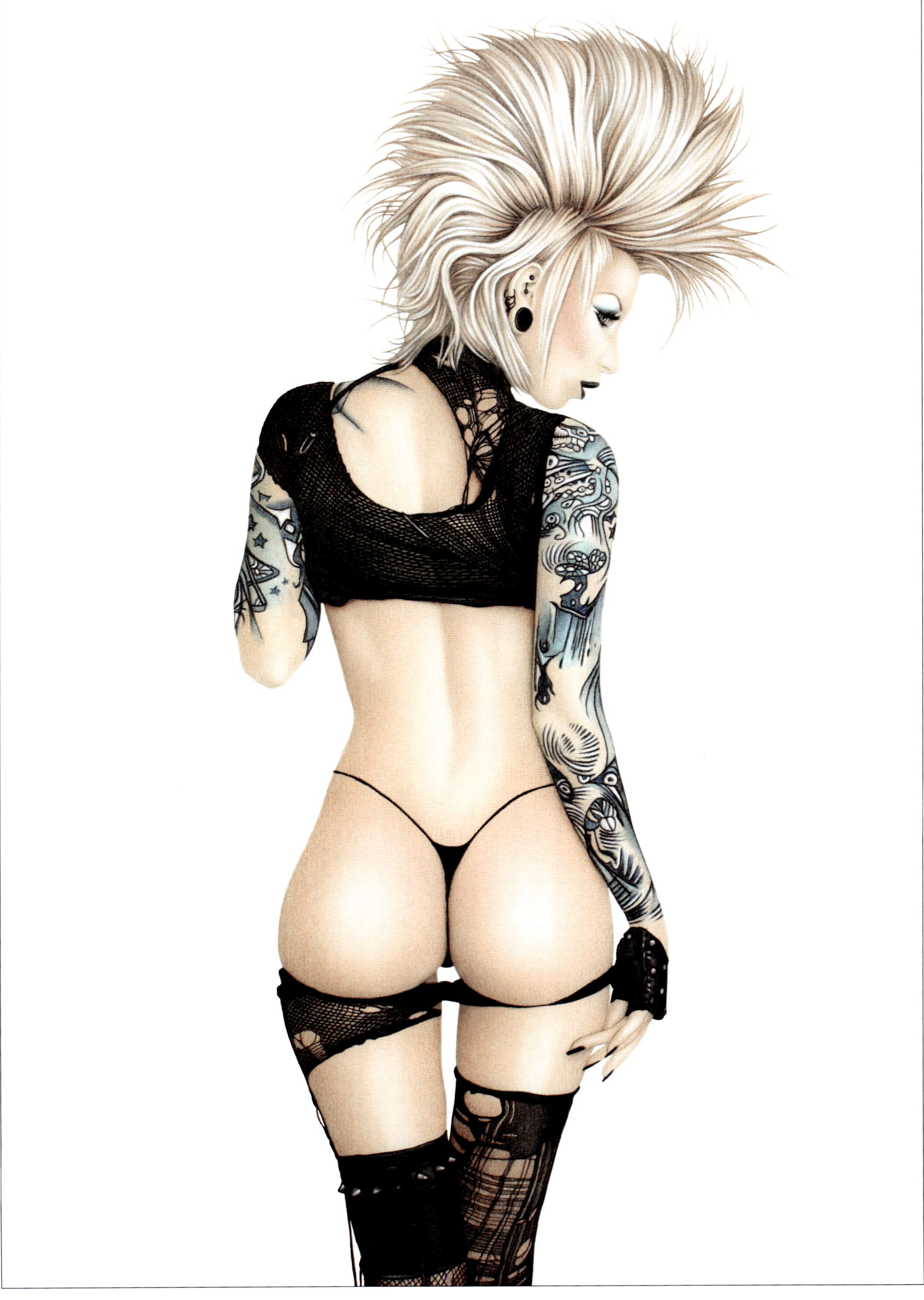

Razor Sharp

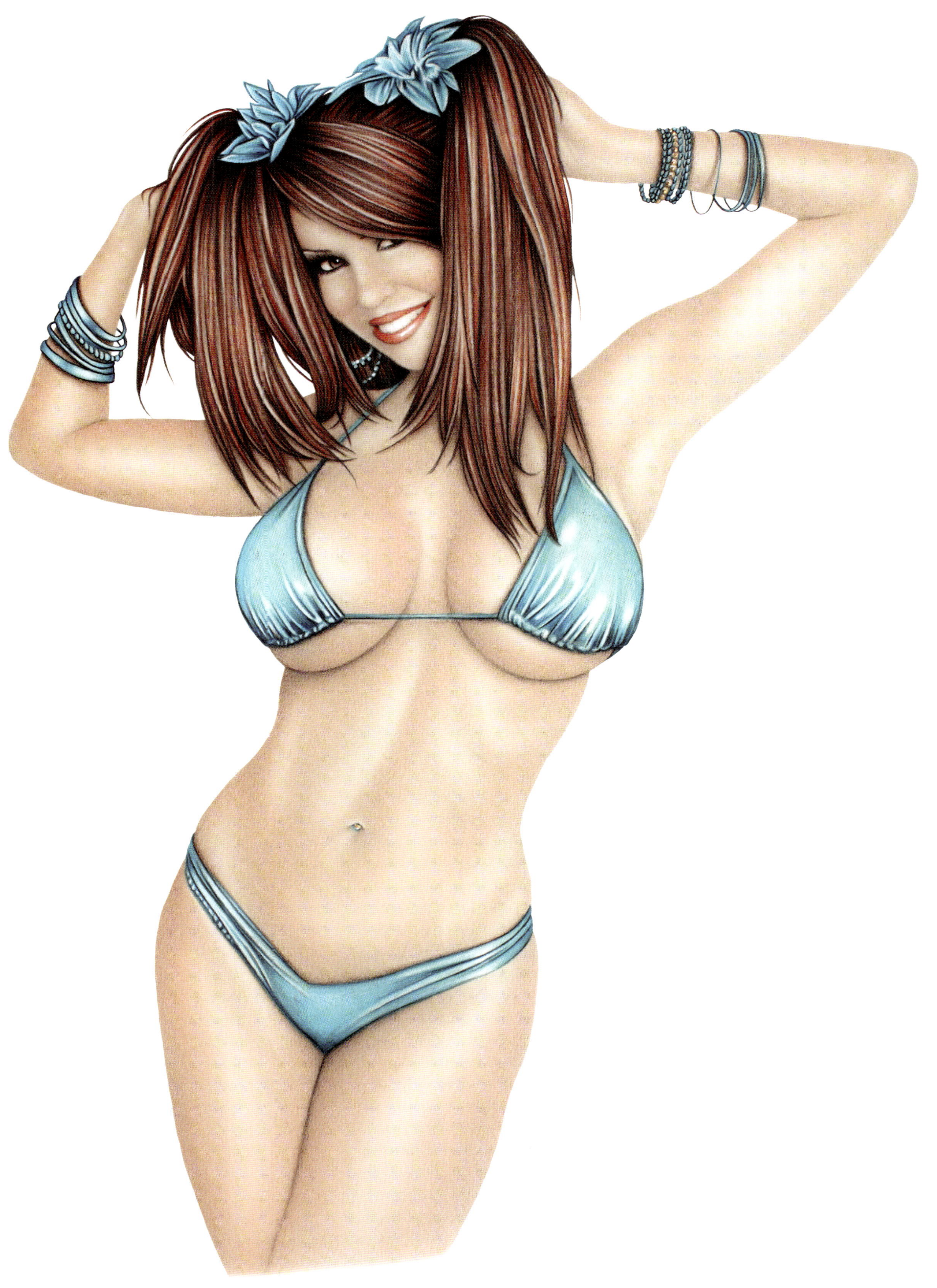

Blue Lotus

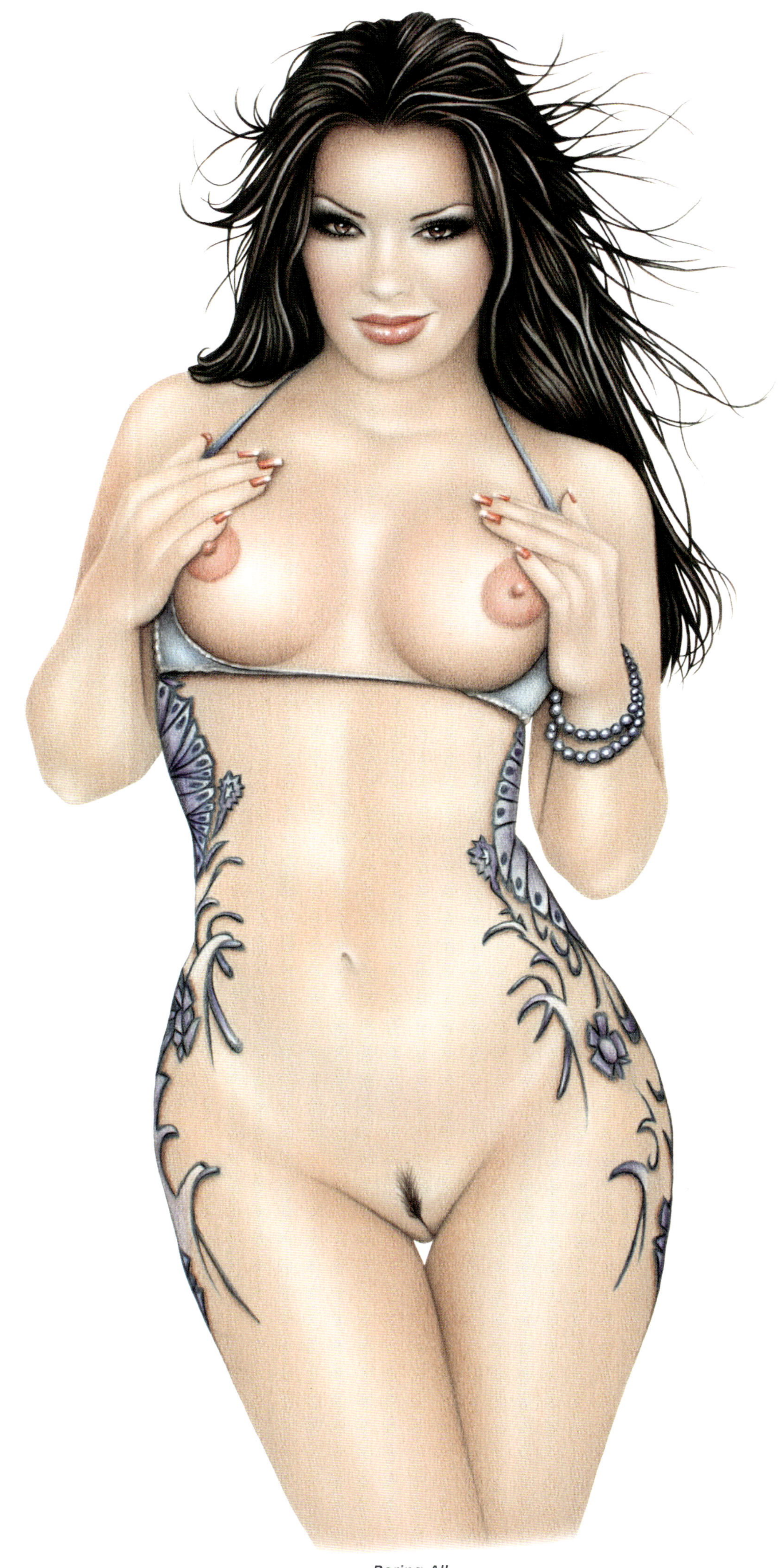

Baring All

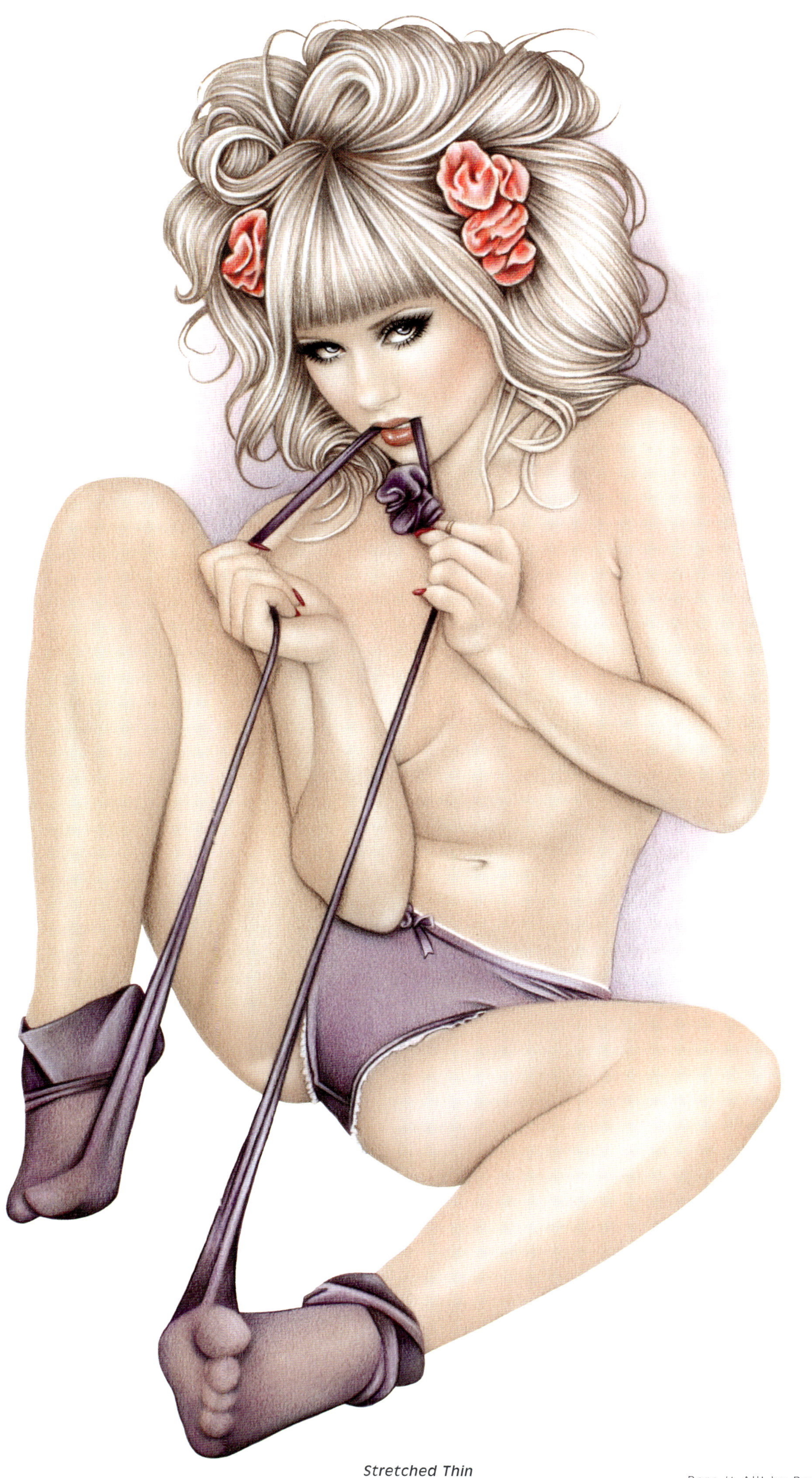

Stretched Thin

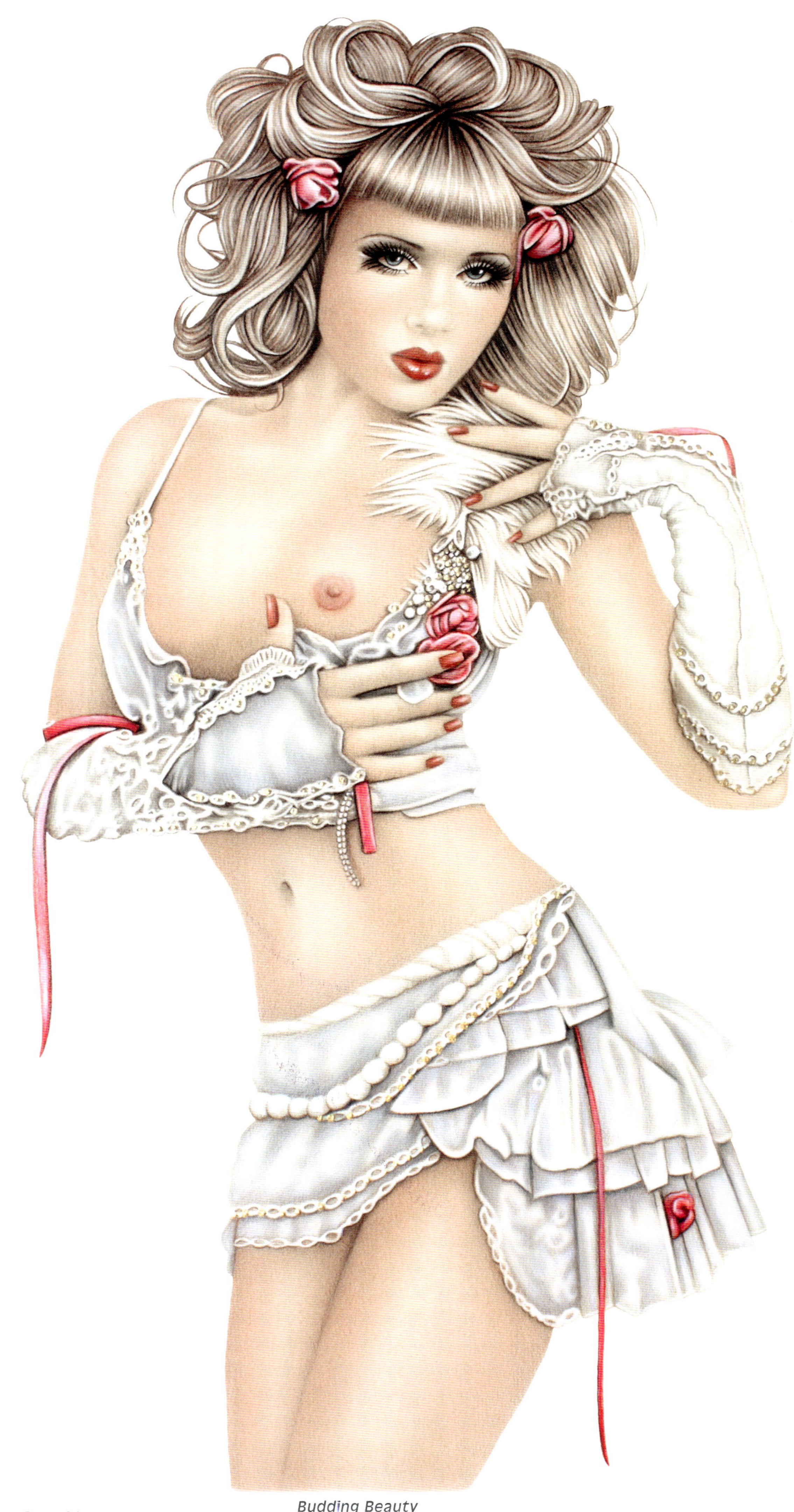

Budding Beauty

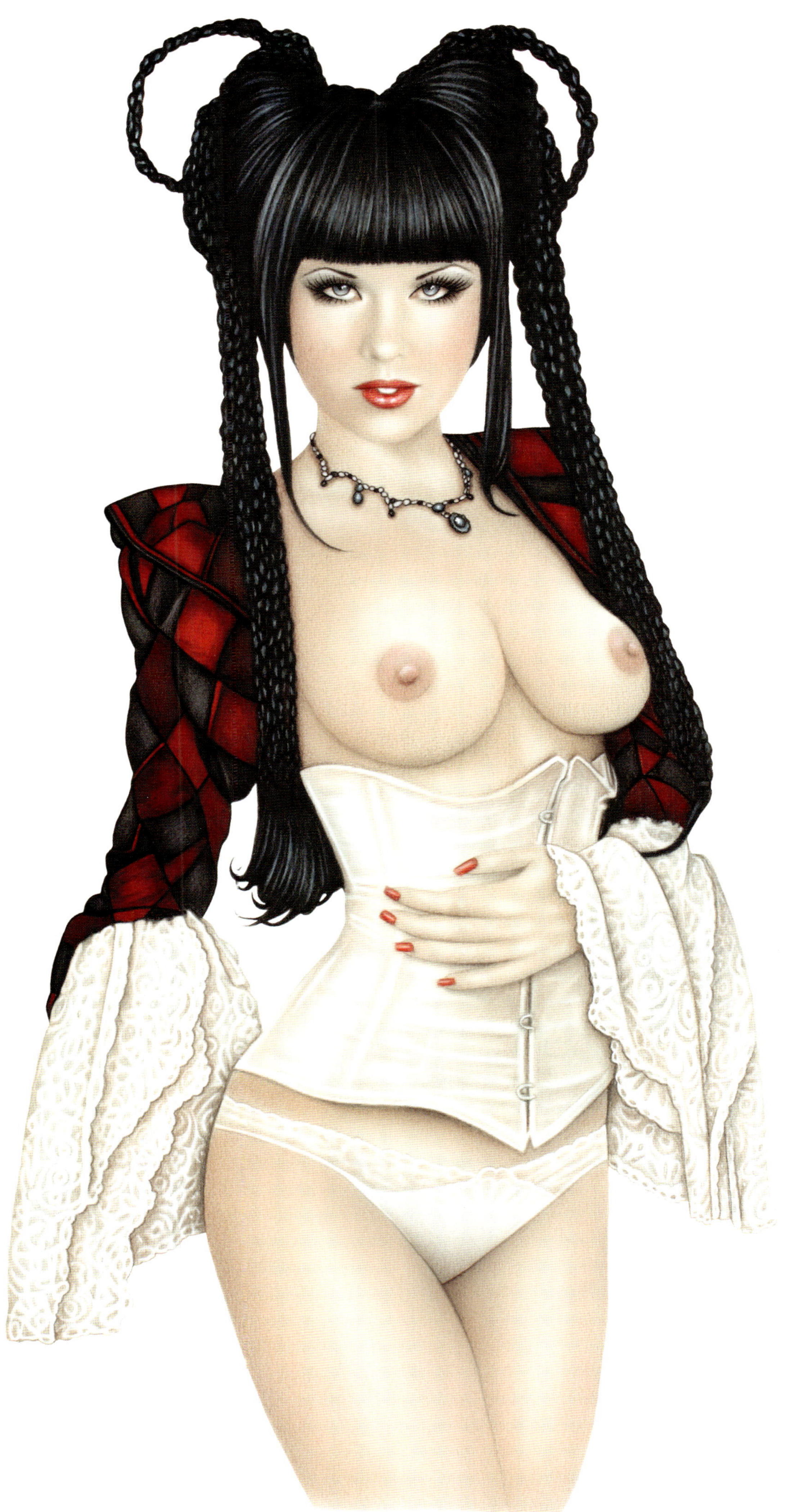

Cyra

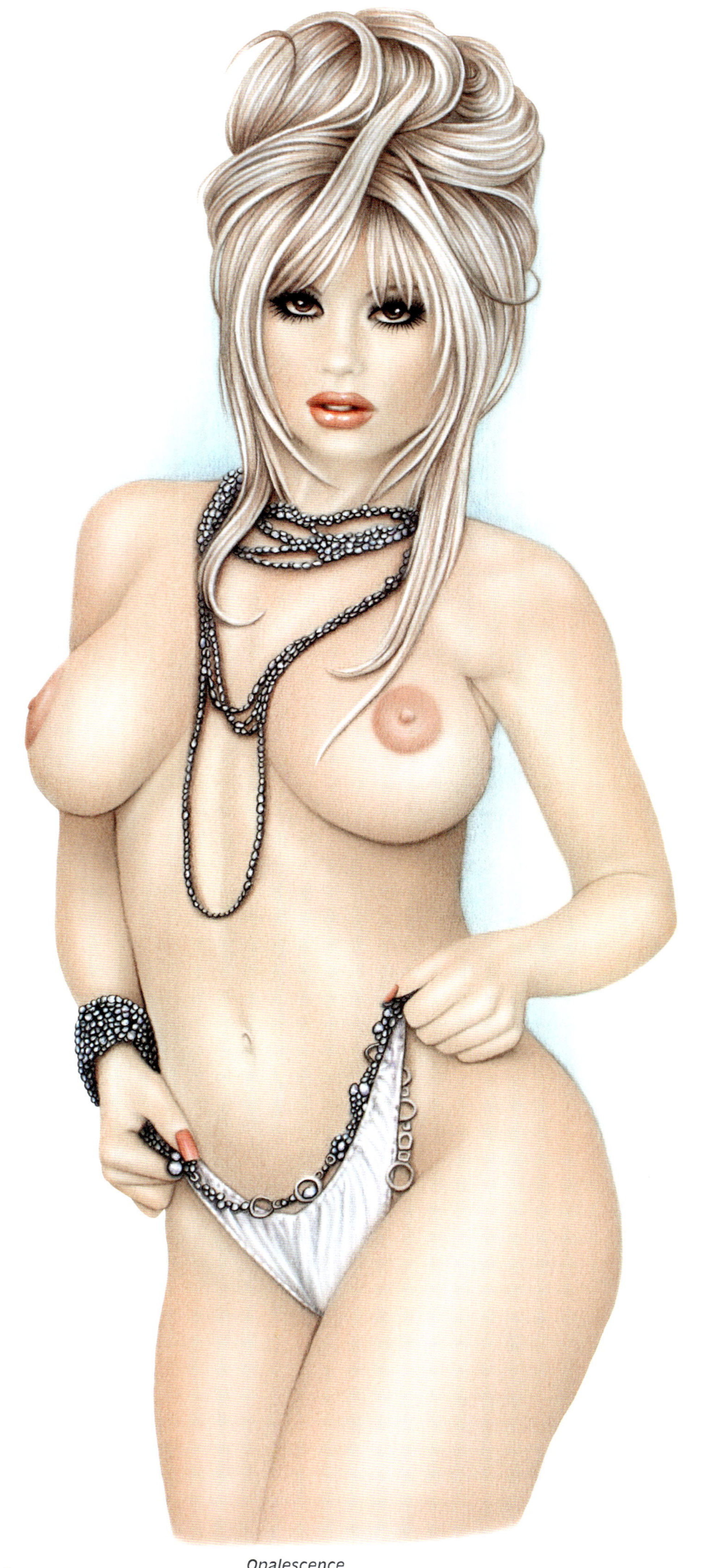

Opalescence

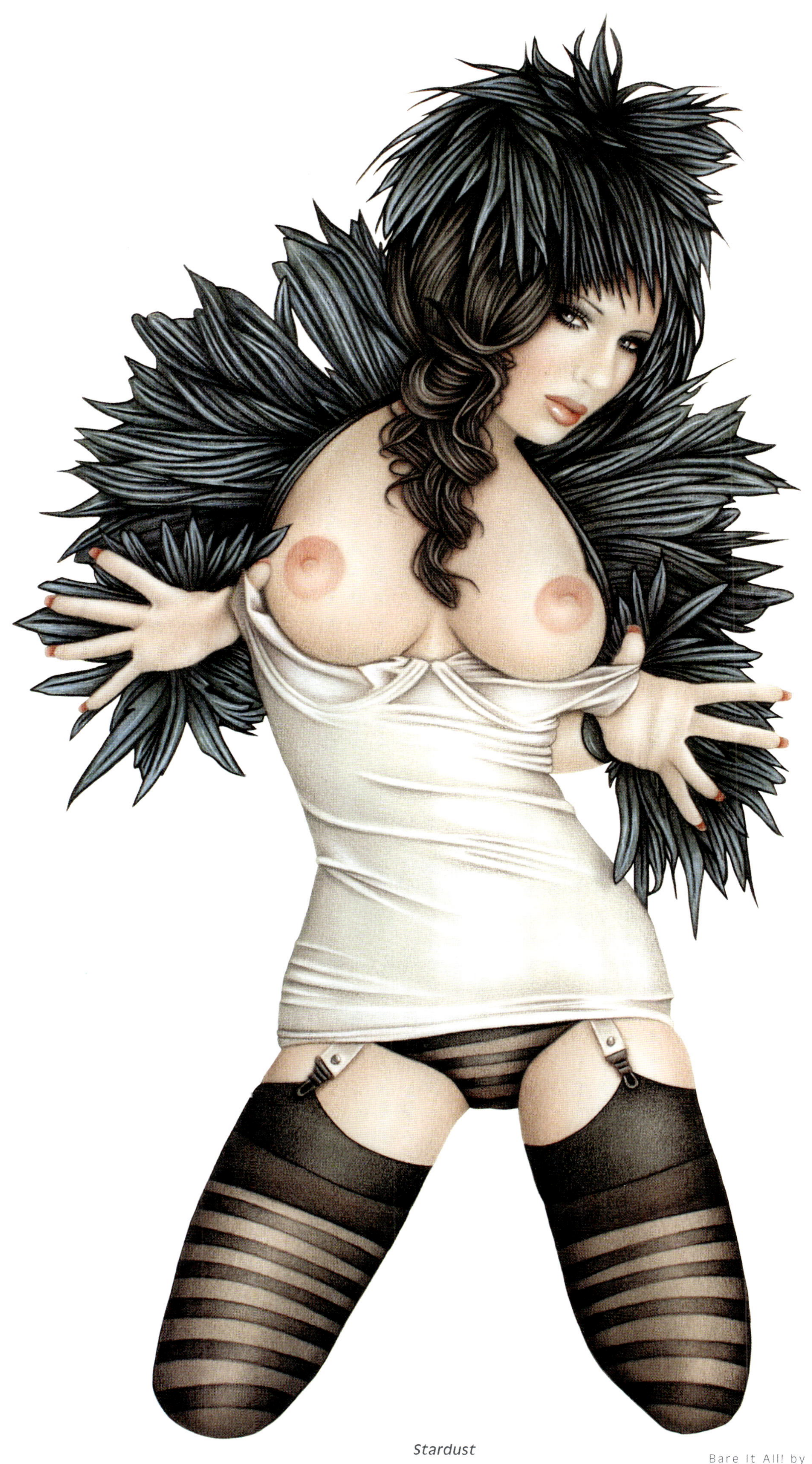

Stardust

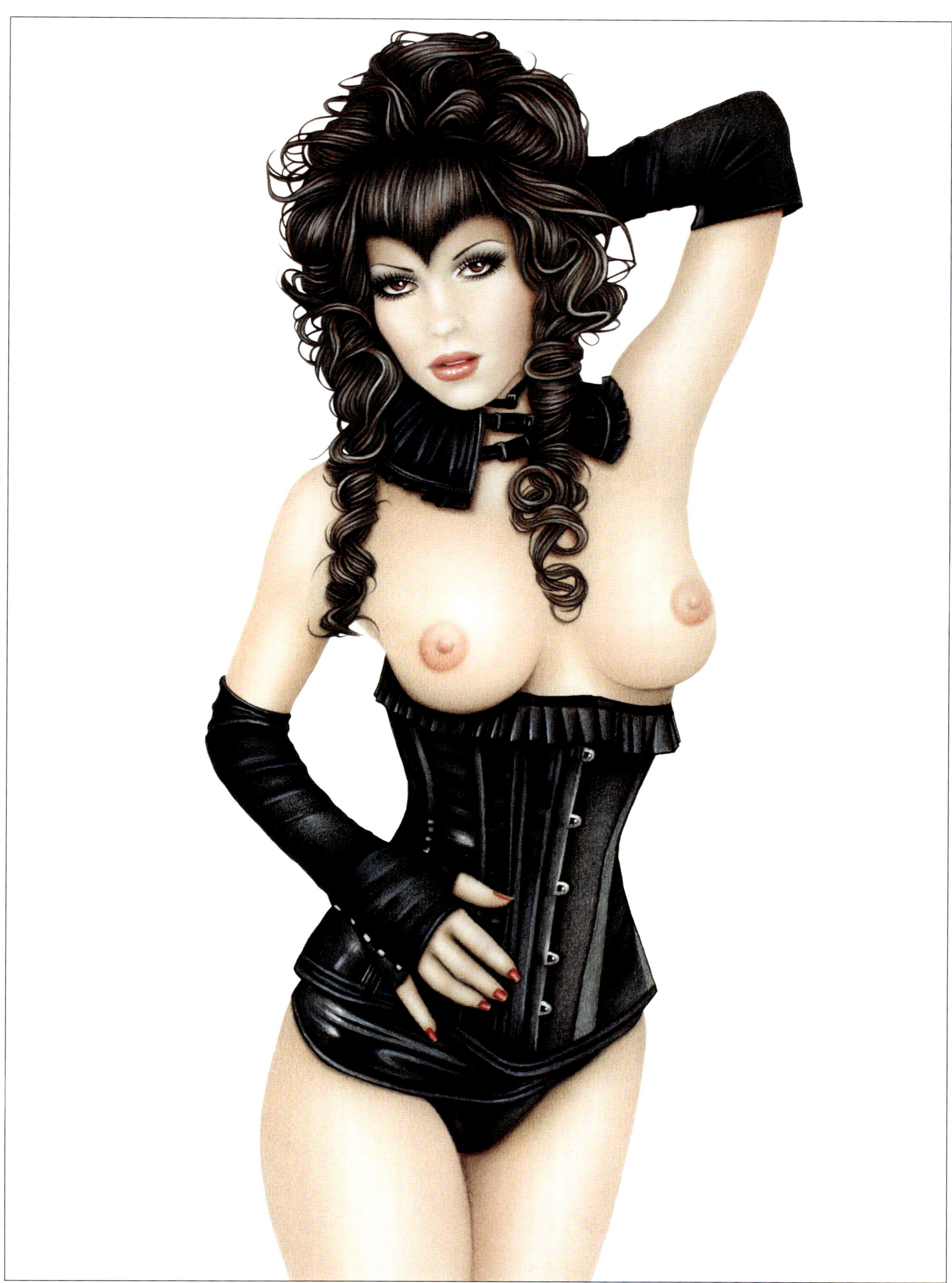

Razor Wired

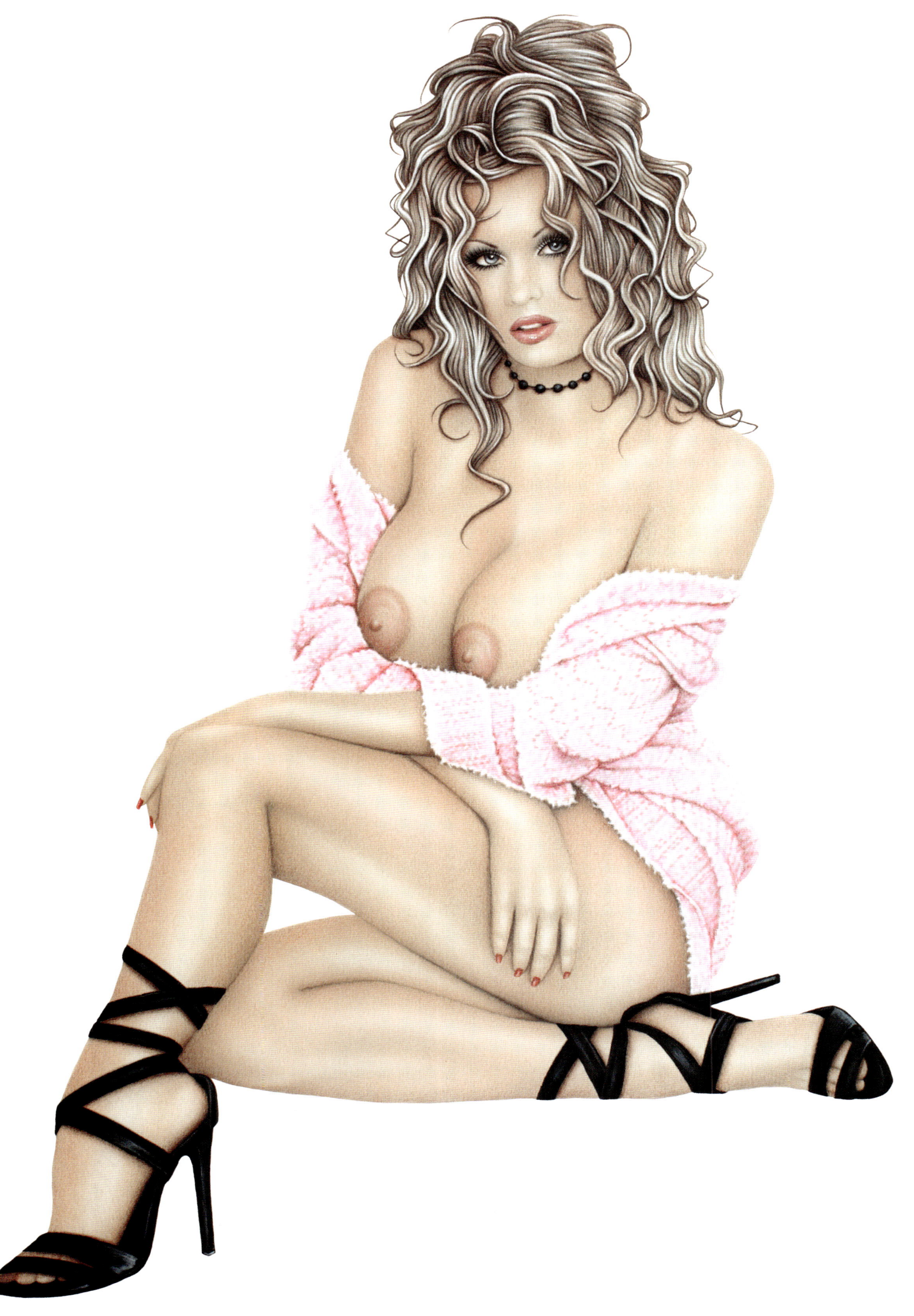

Warm Fuzzies

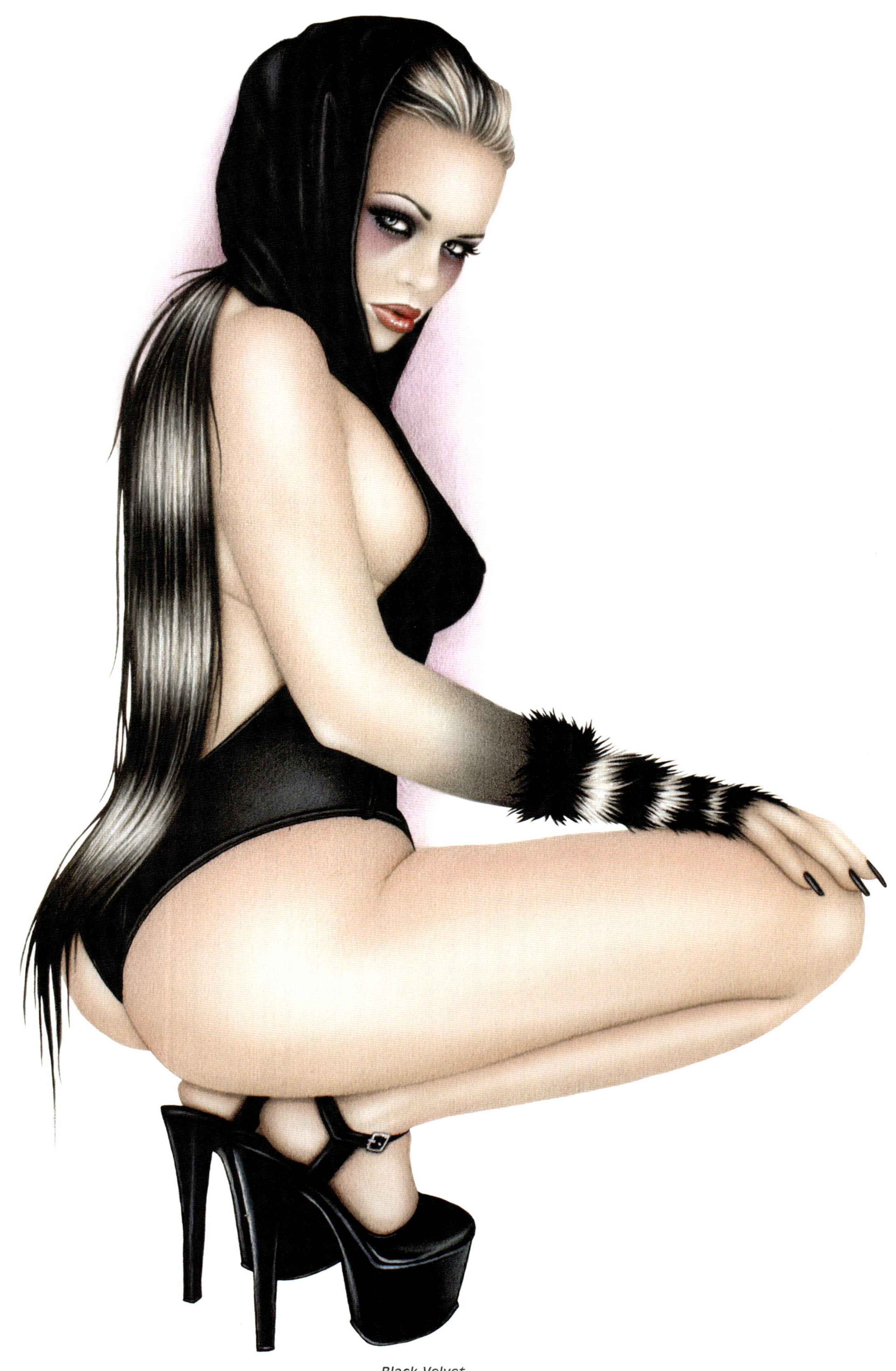

Black Velvet

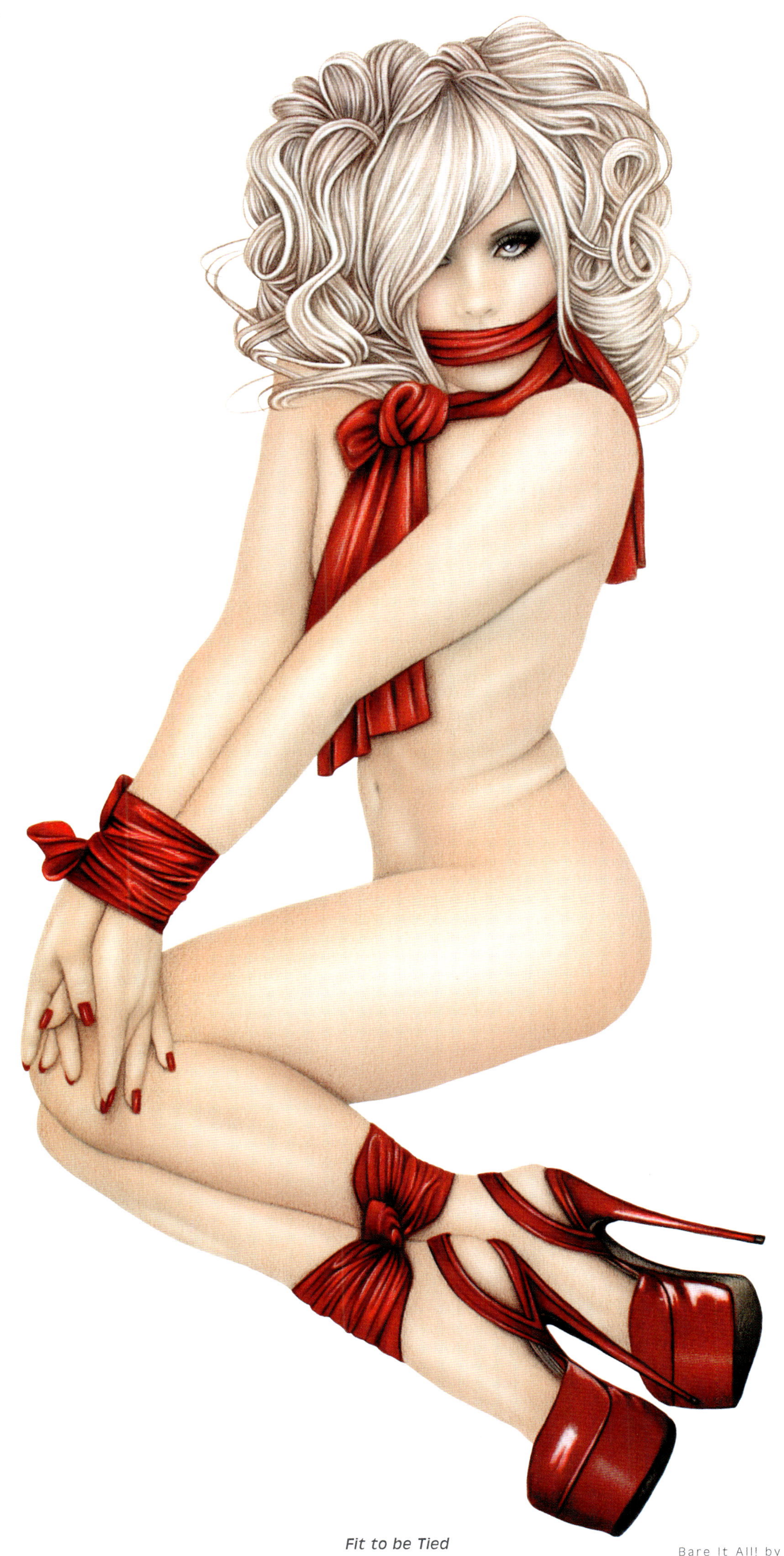

Fit to be Tied

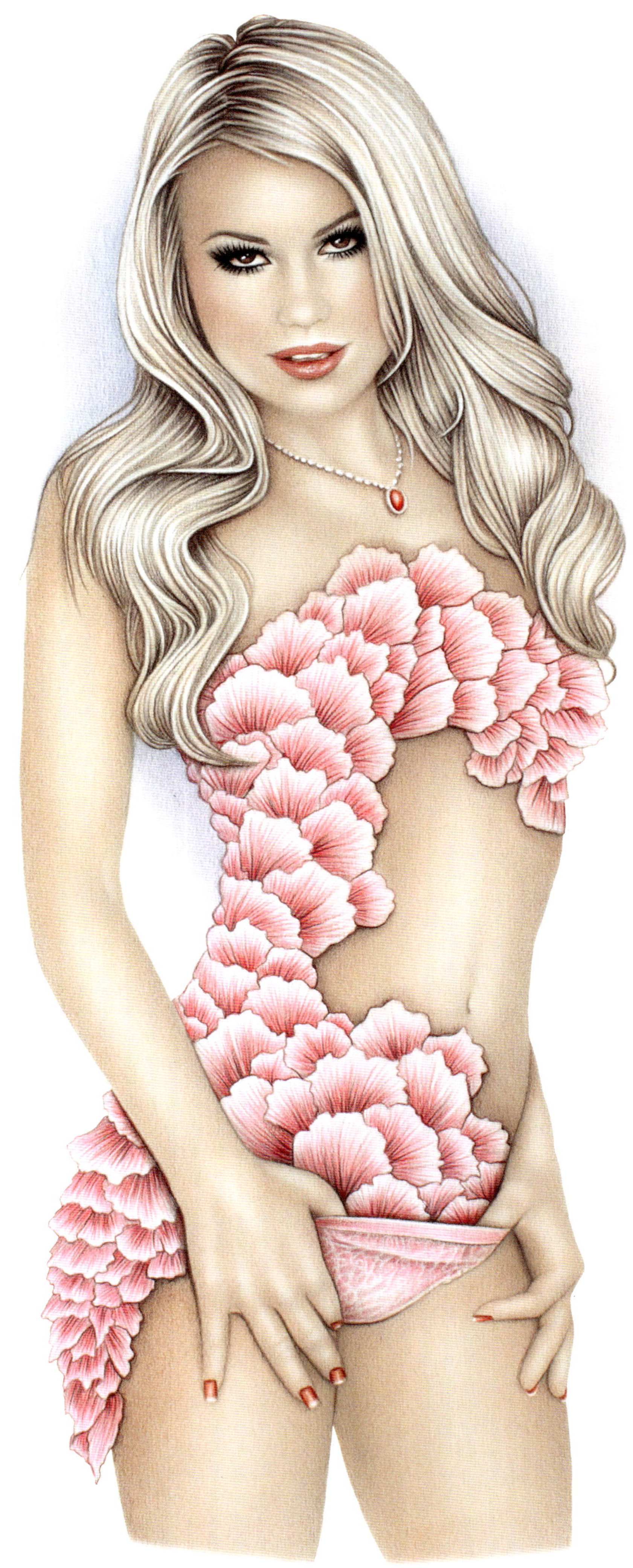

Spring Fever

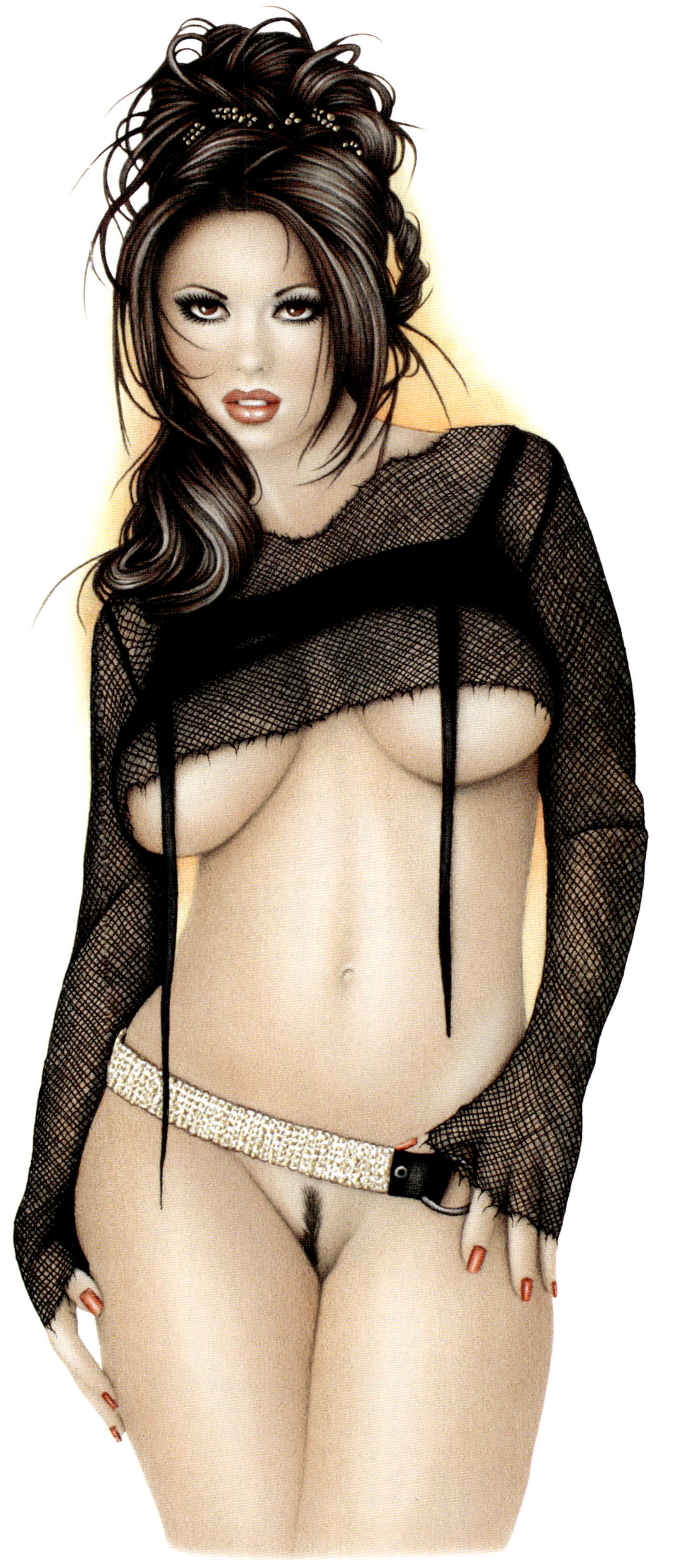

Fringe

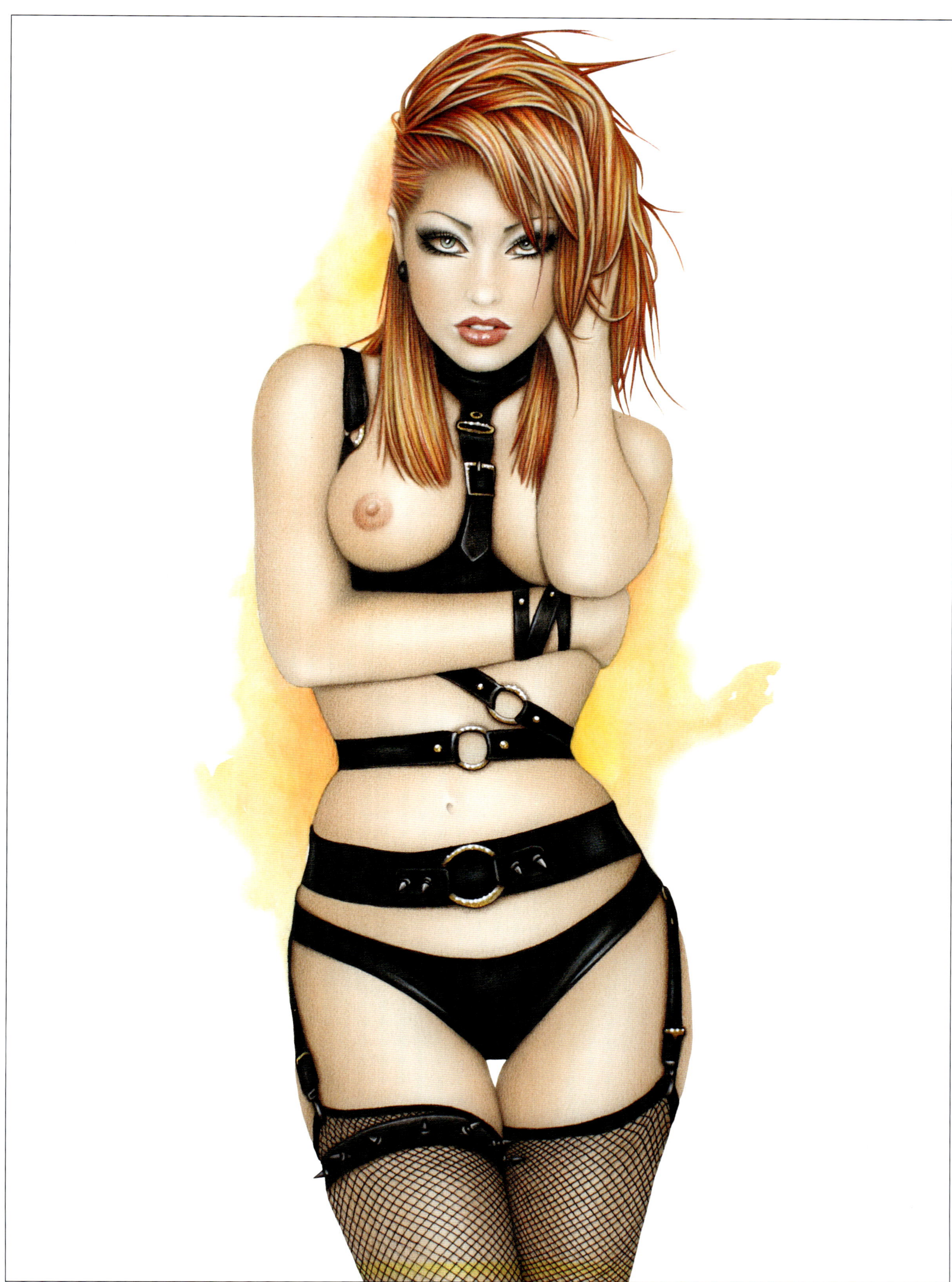

Rusty Nail

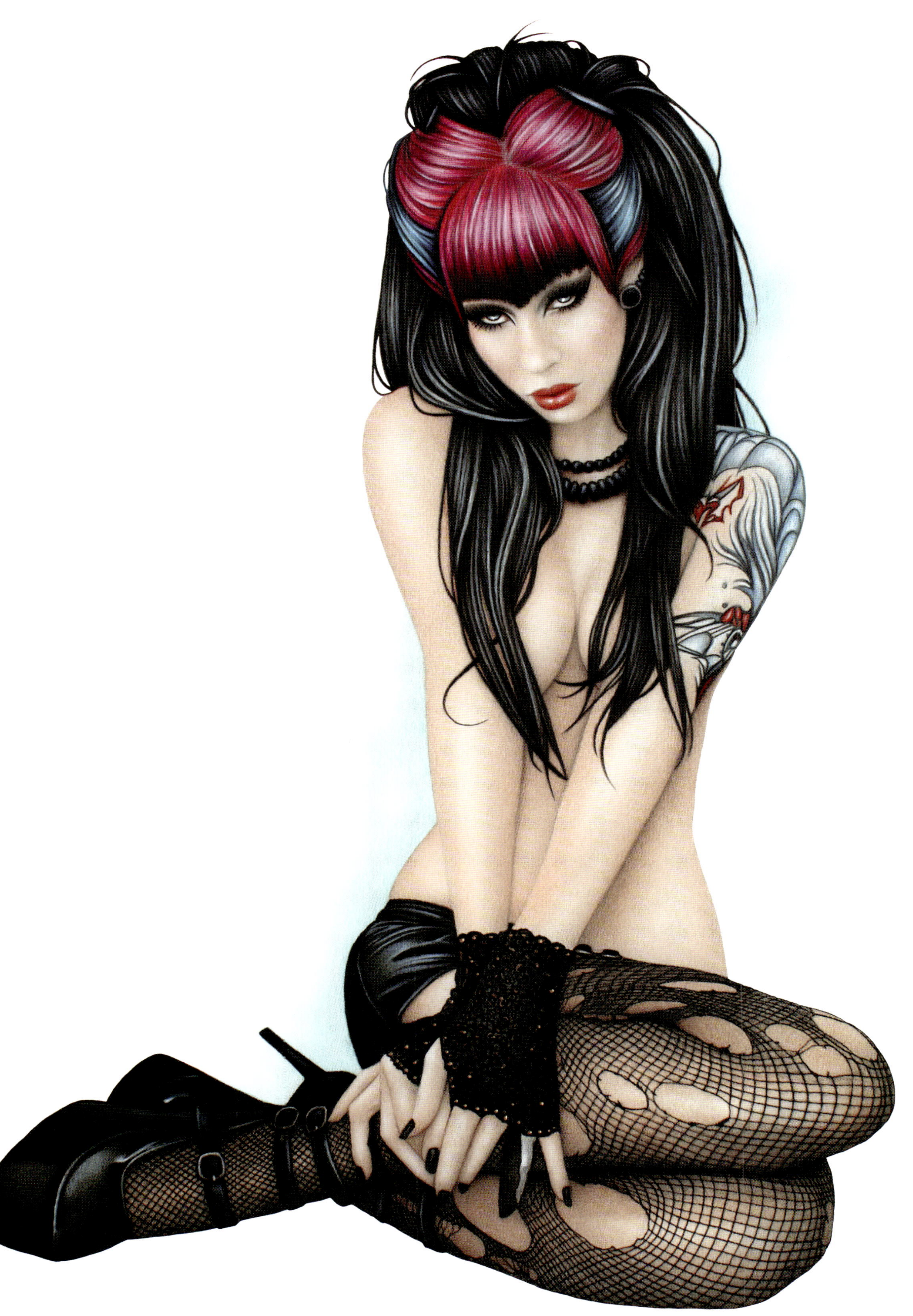

Razor's Edge

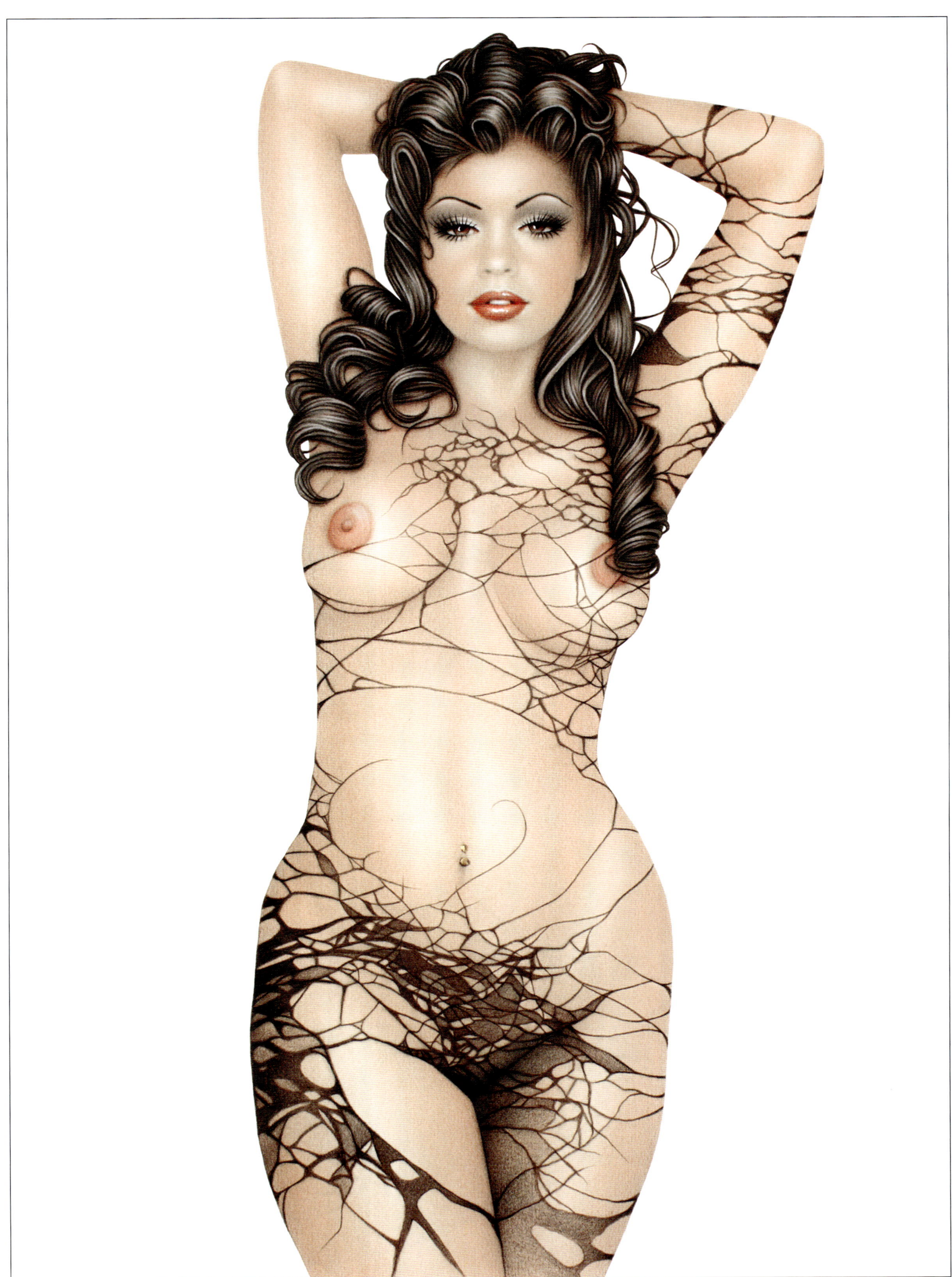

Labyrinth

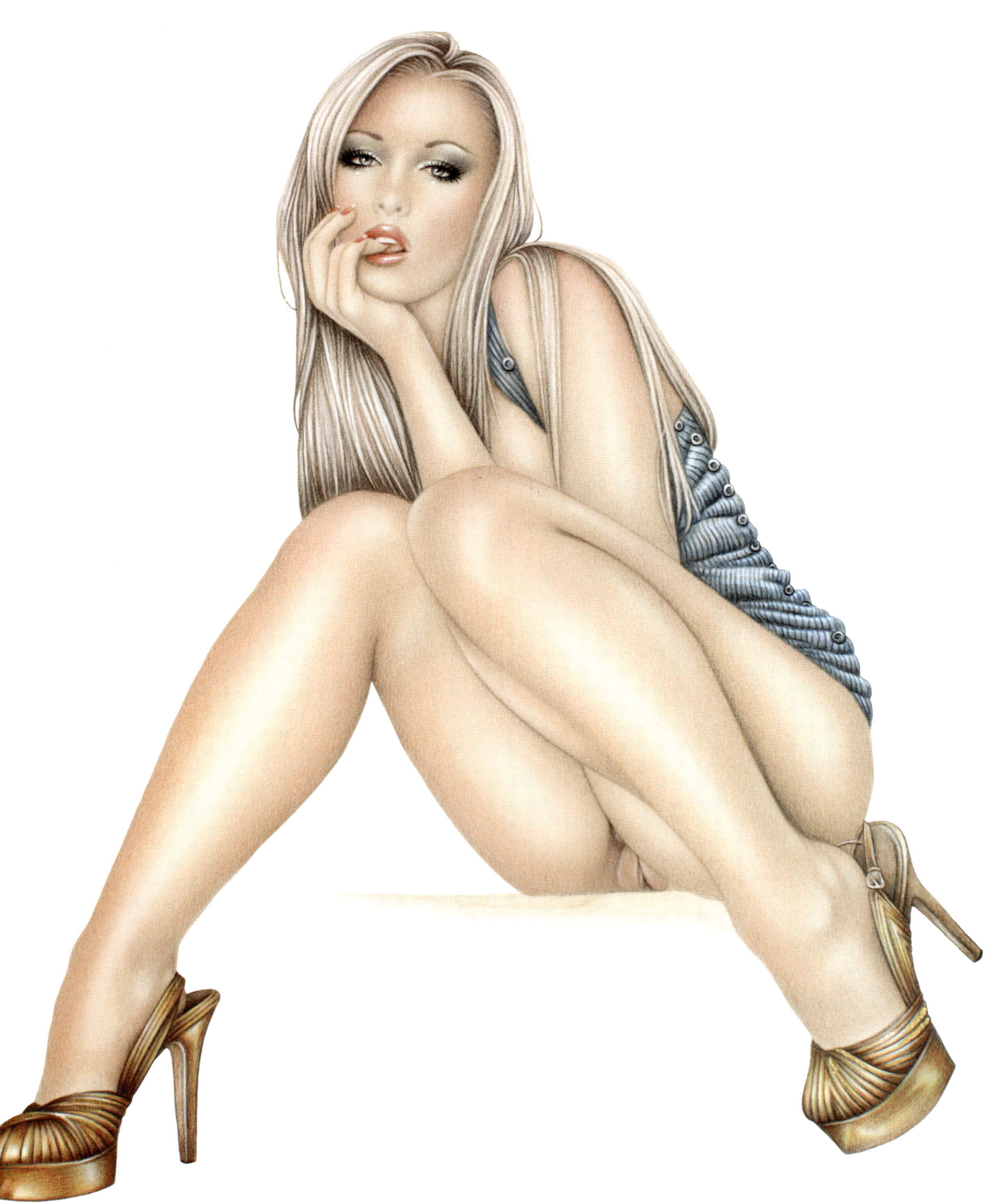

Wonder Lust

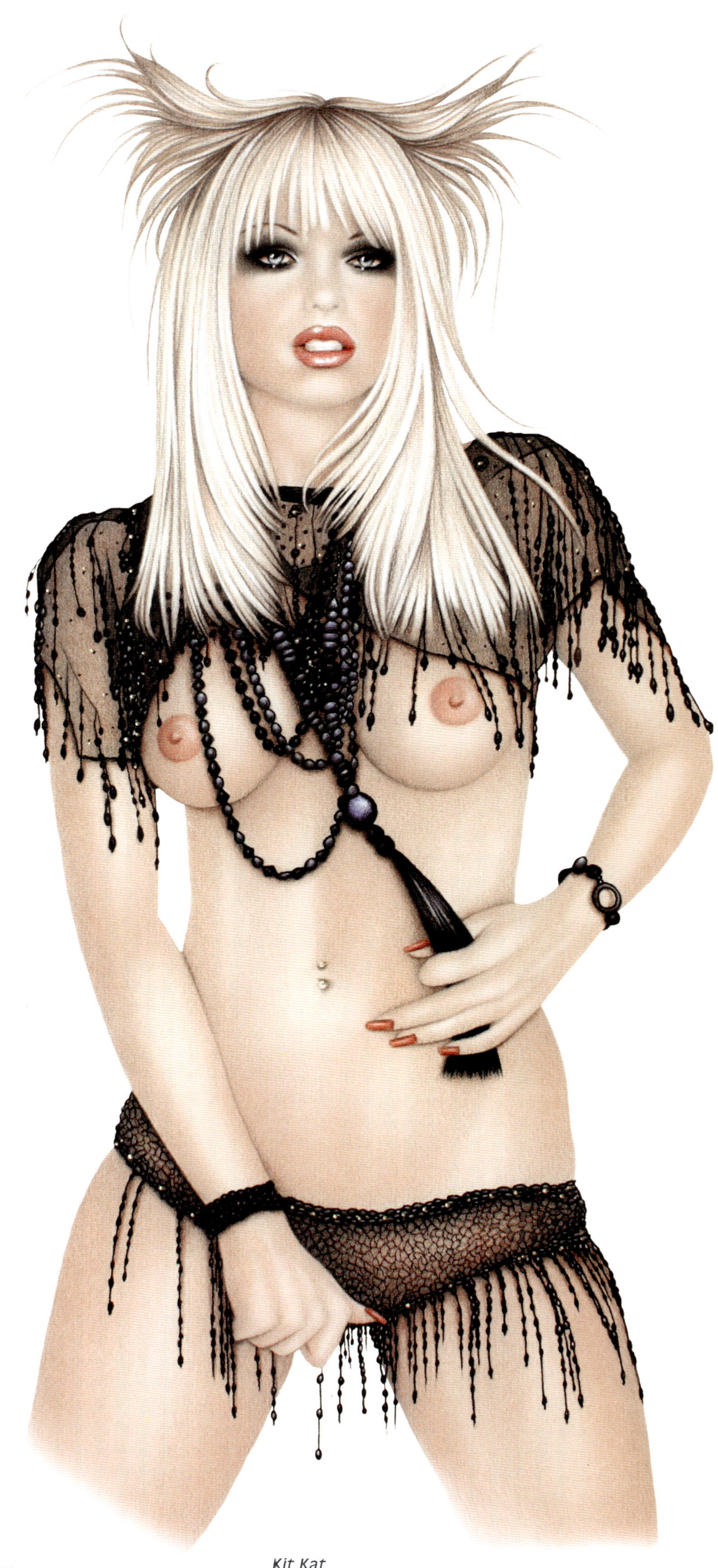

Kit Kat

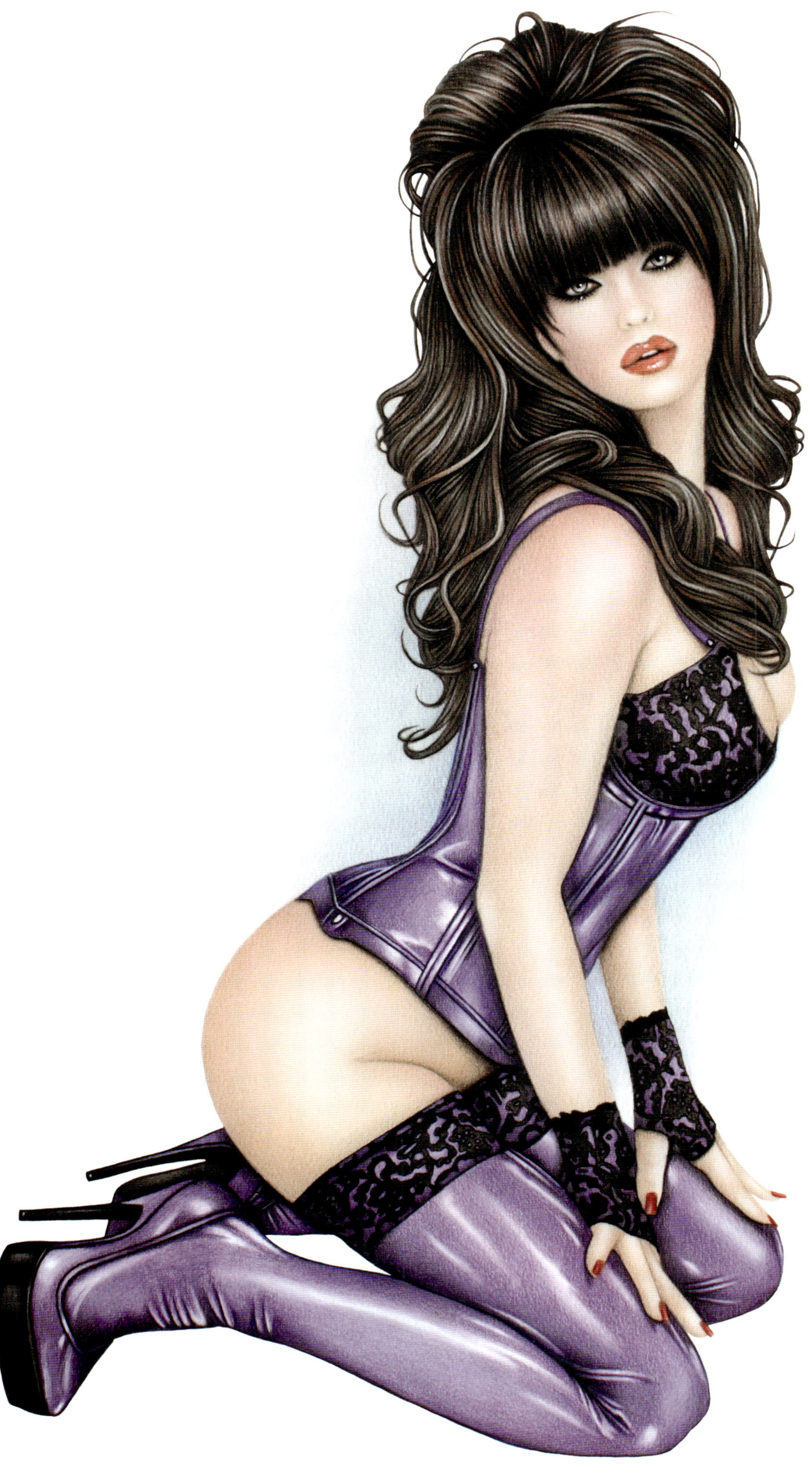

Violette

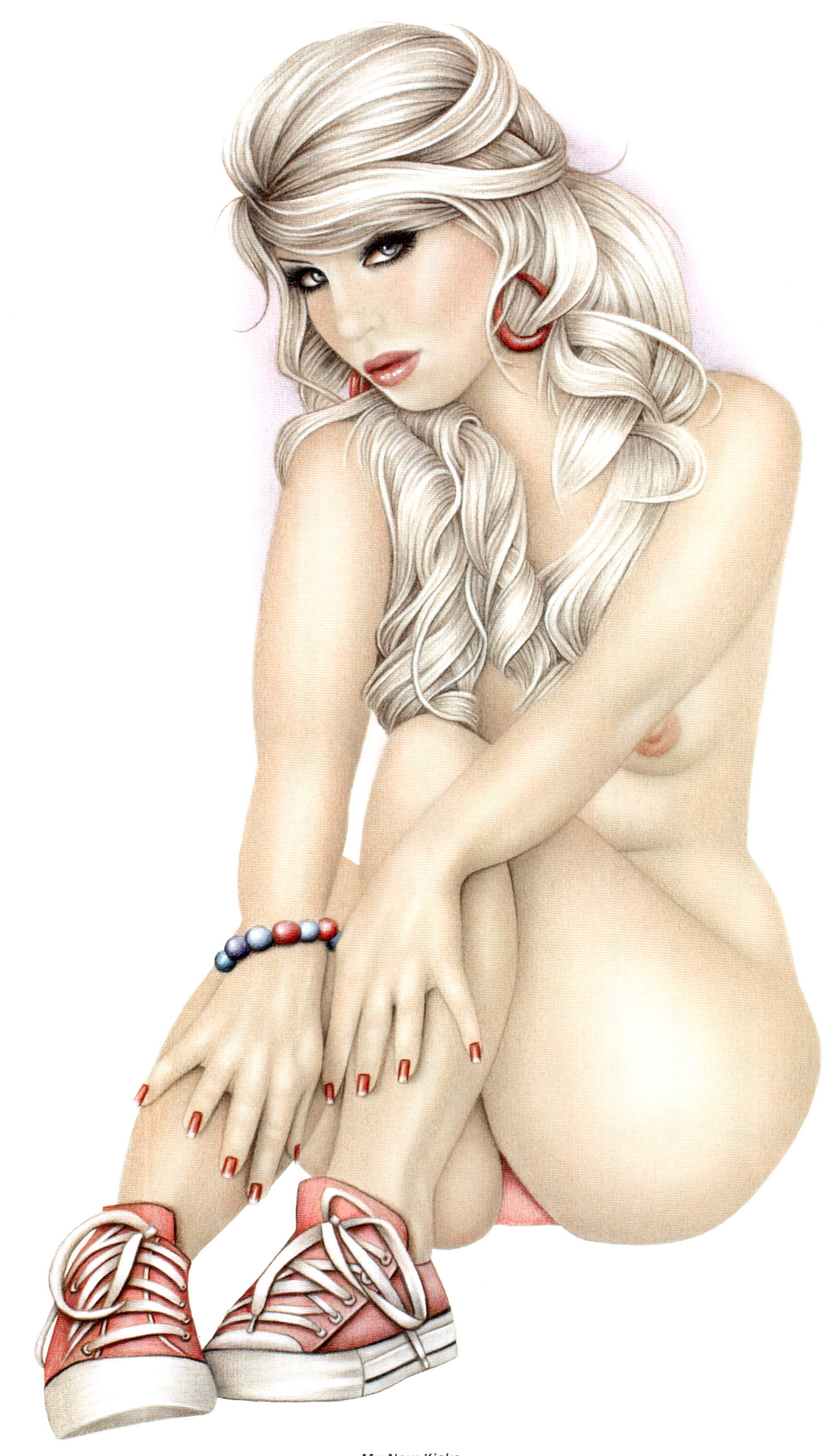

My New Kicks

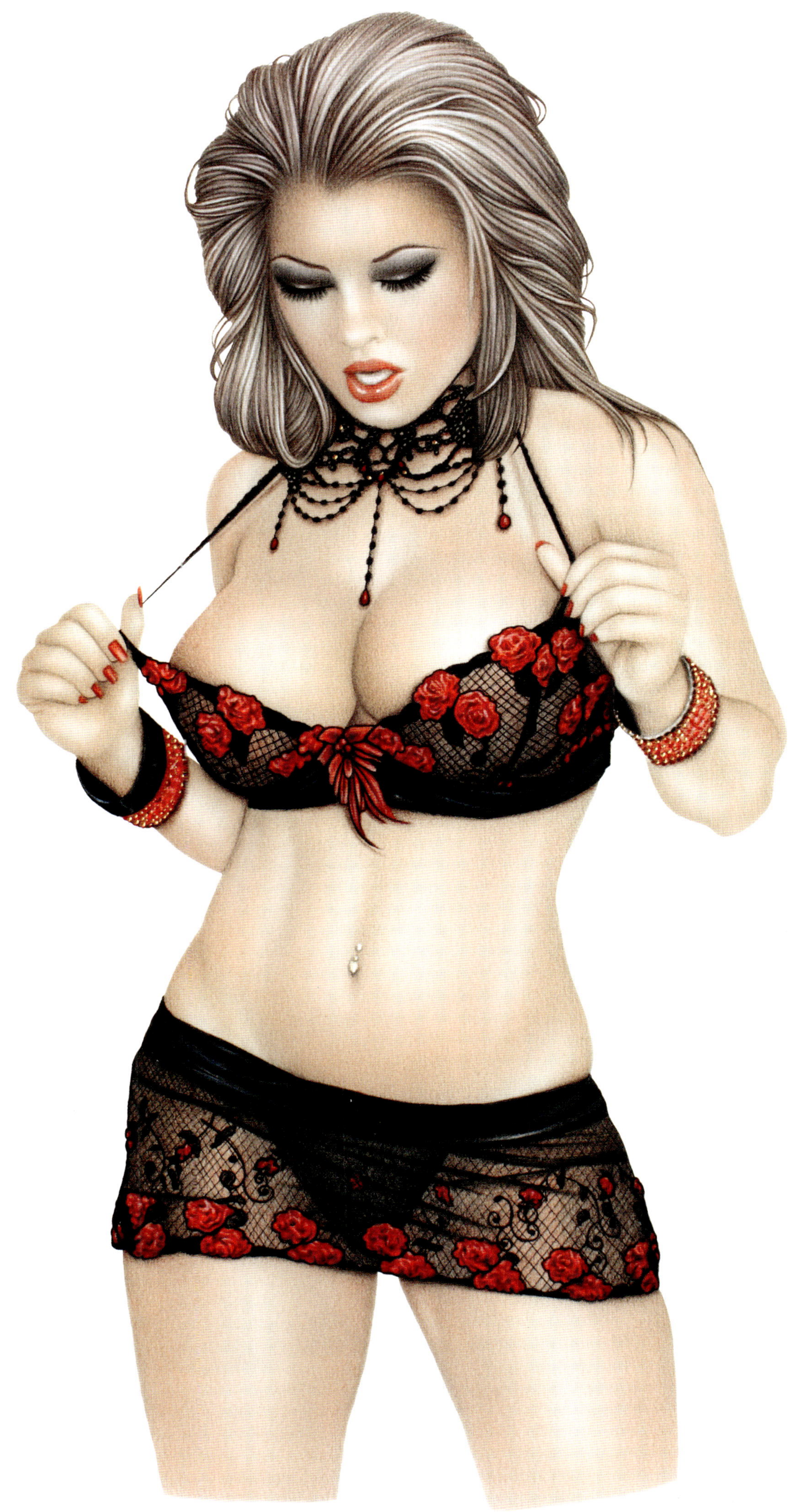

Rosette

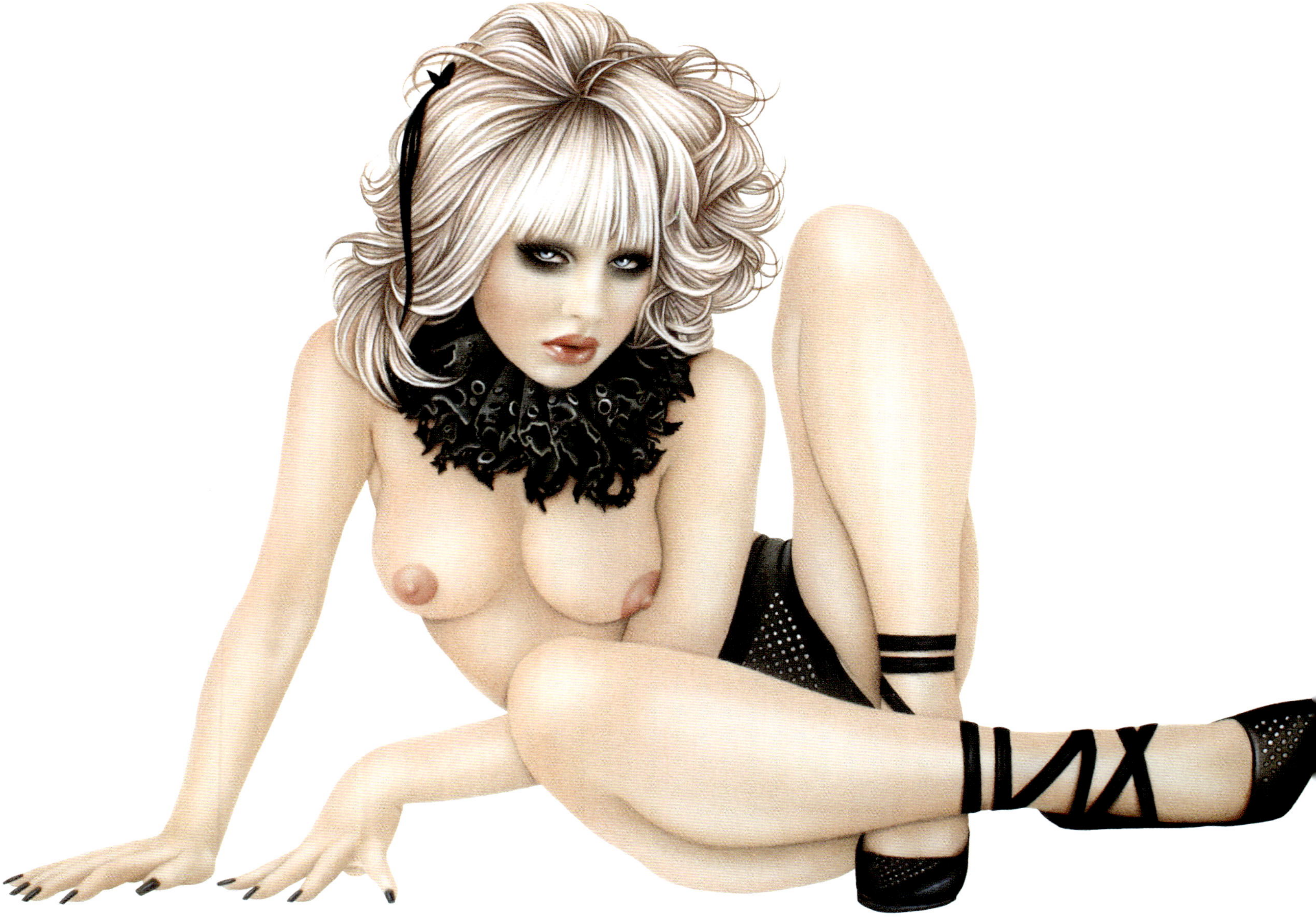

Twisted Sister

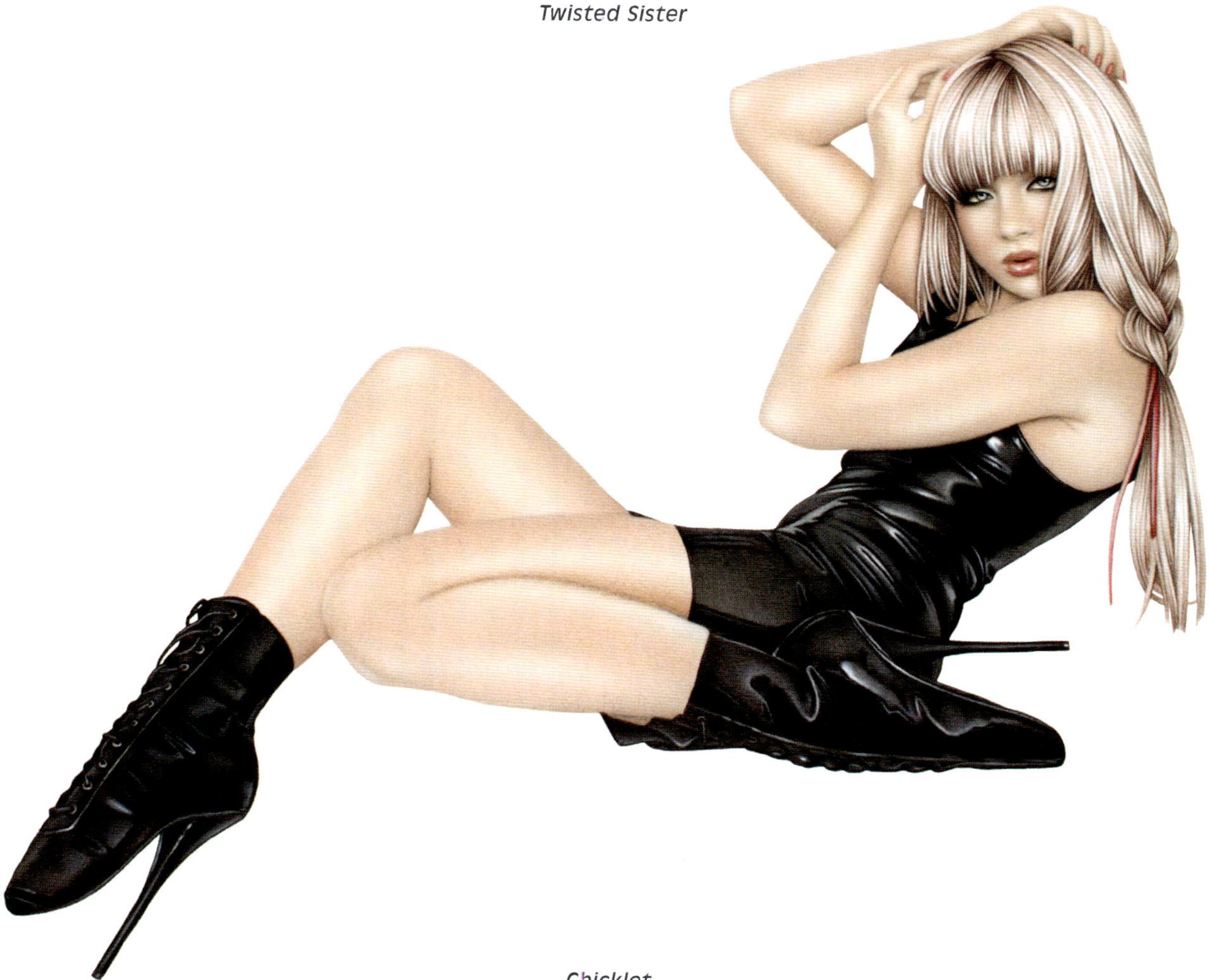

Chicklet

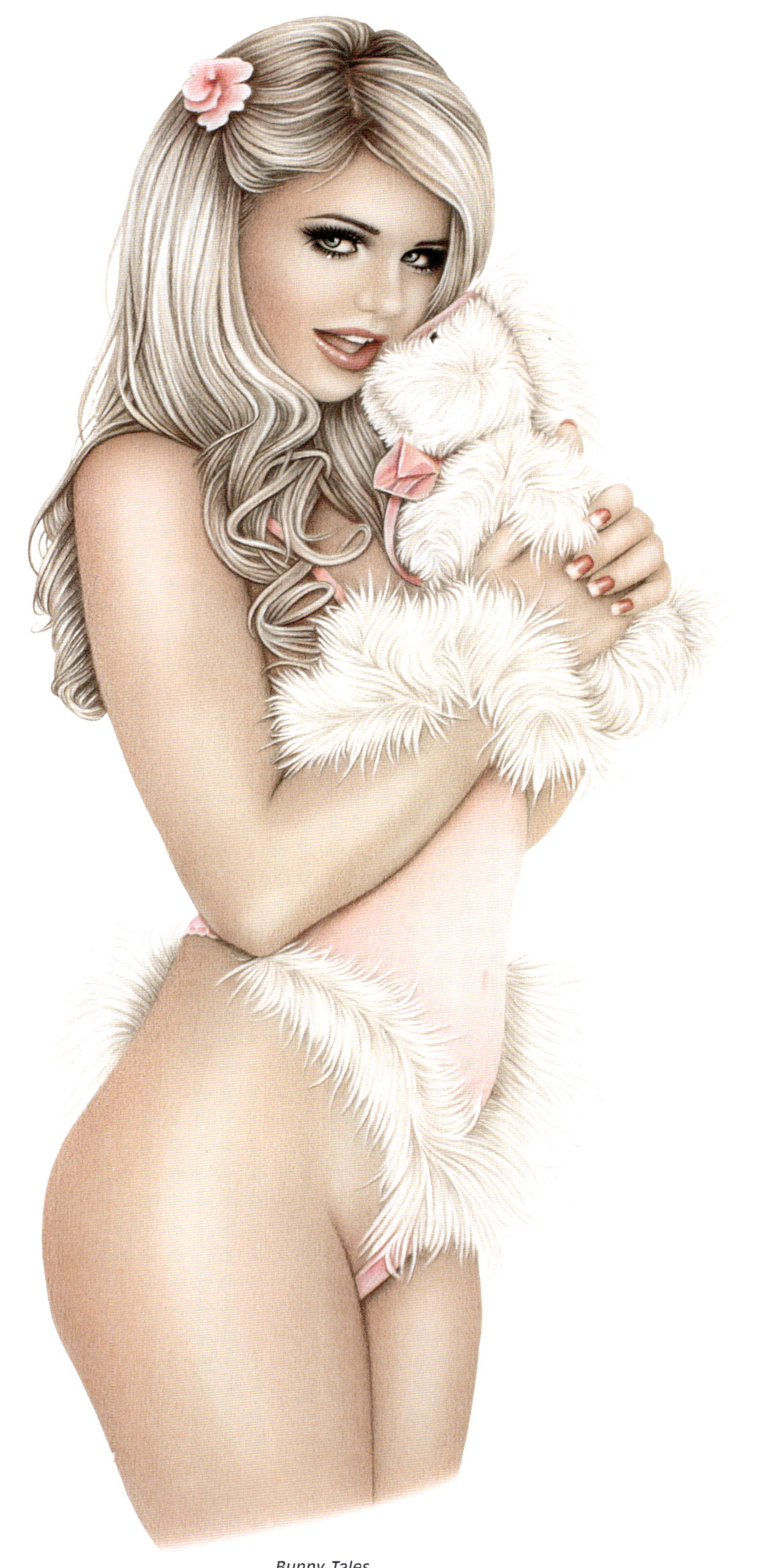

Bunny Tales

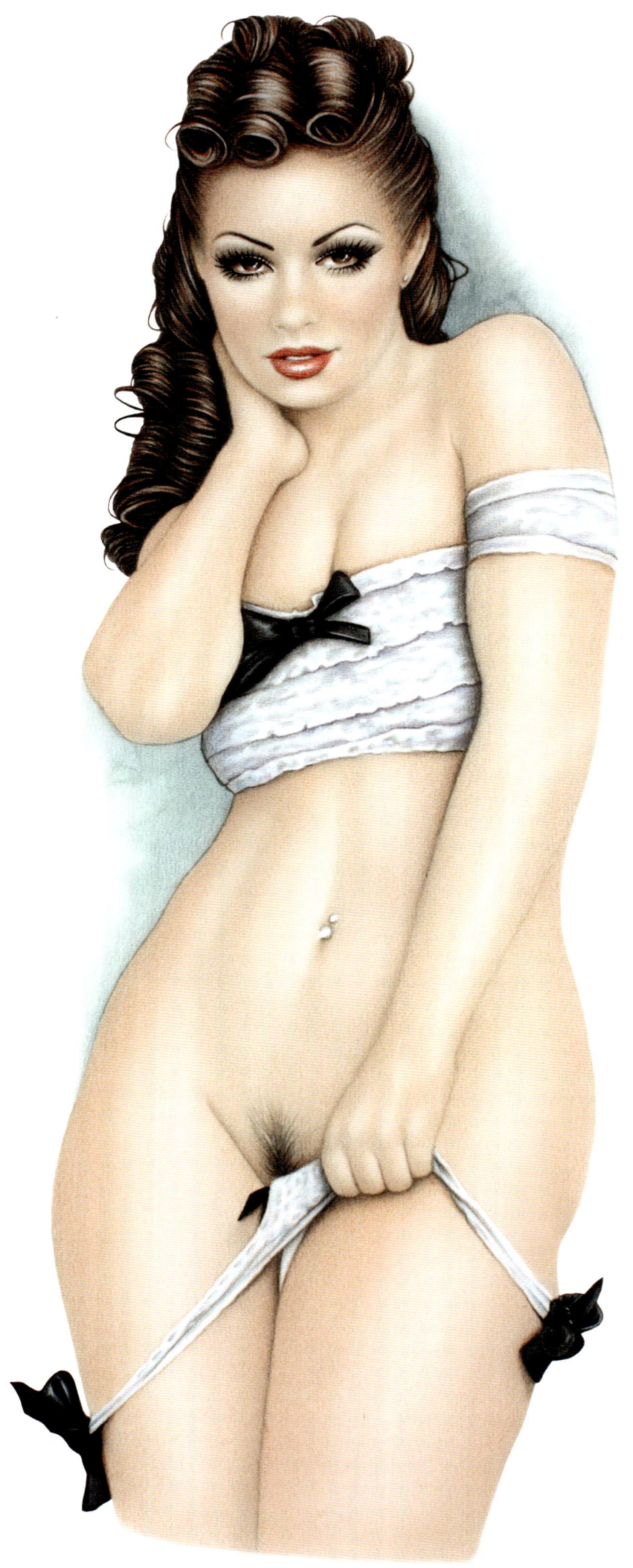

Timeless Beauty

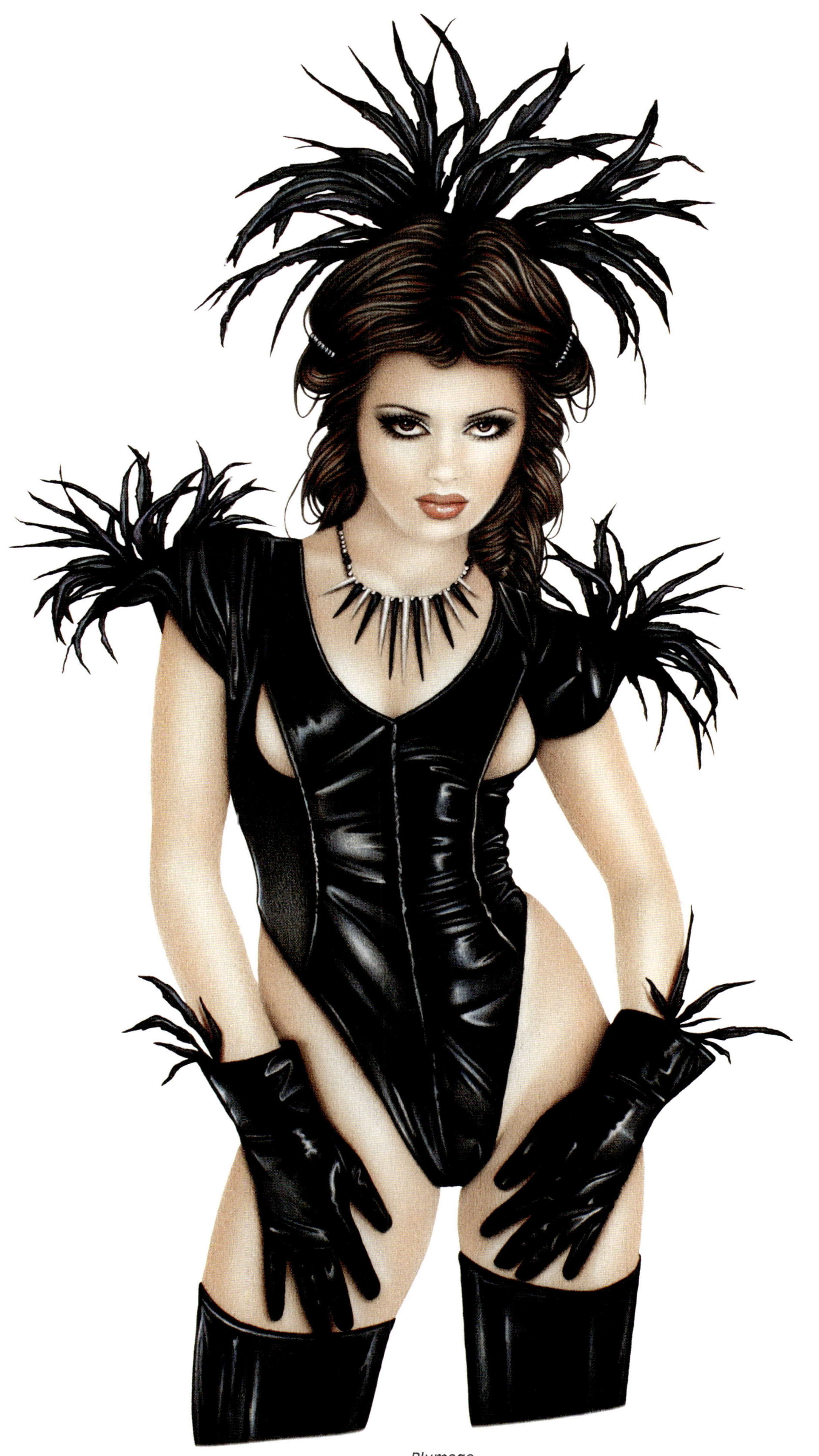

Plumage

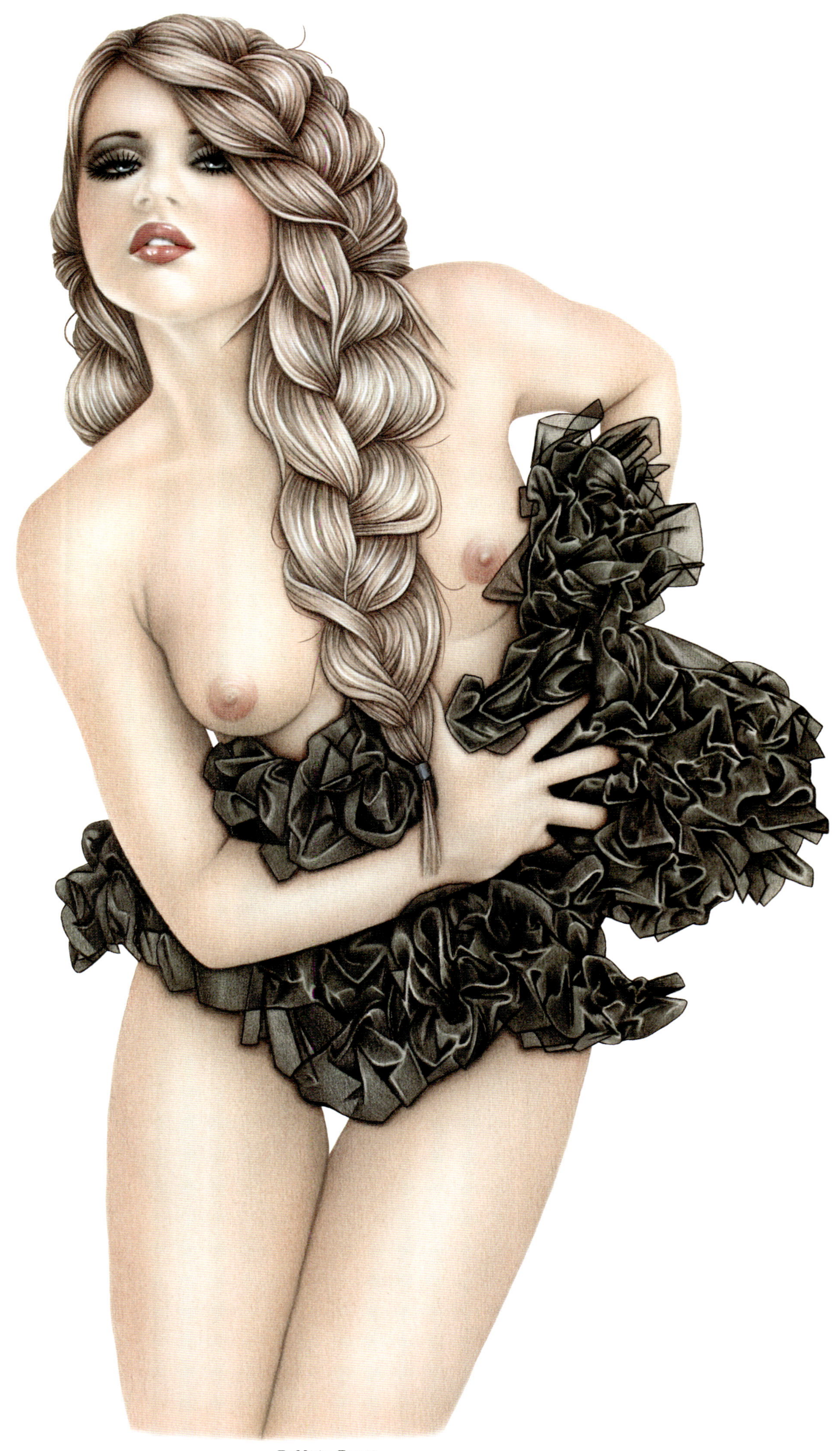

Taffeta Tease

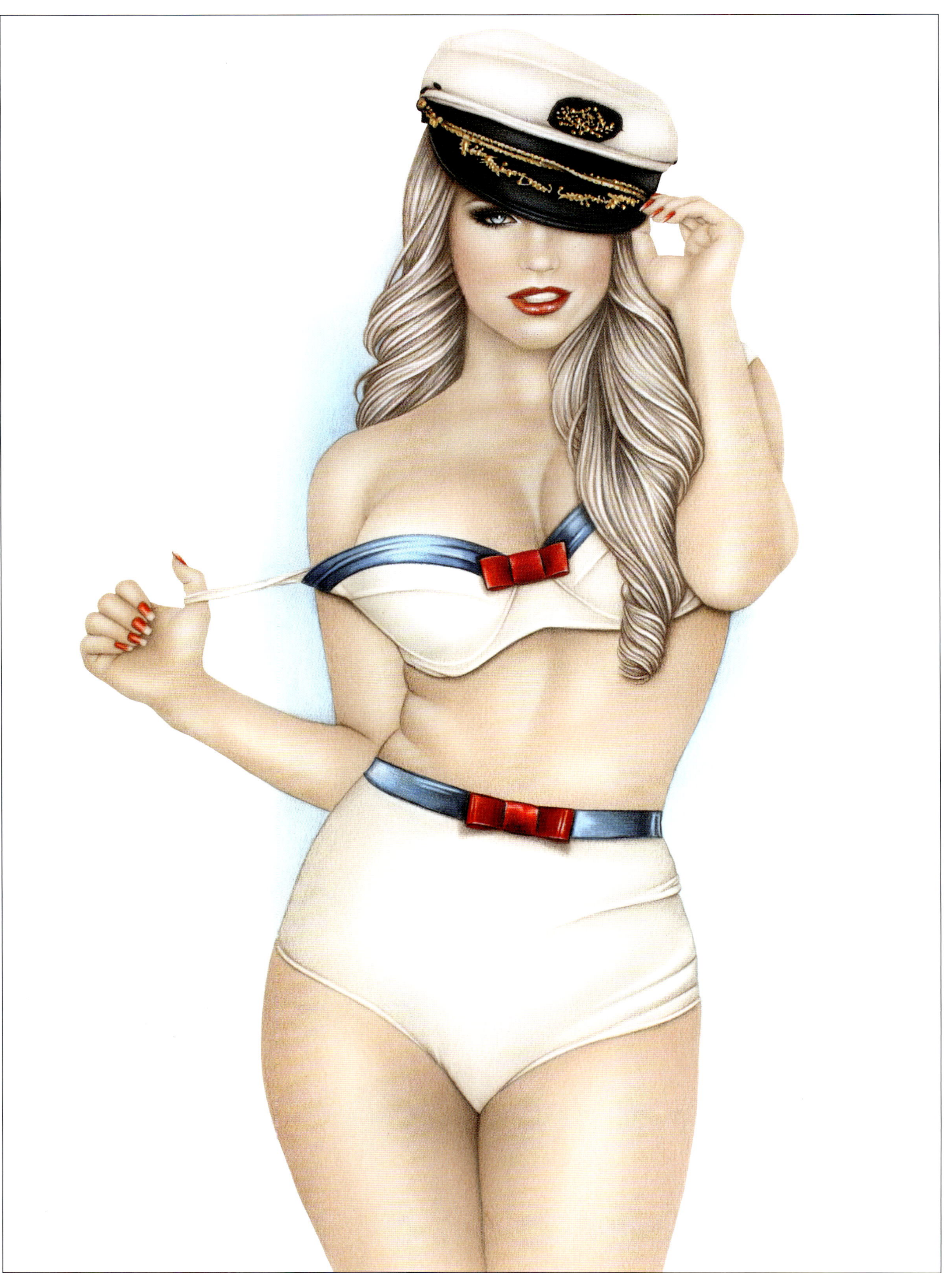

Sea Worthy

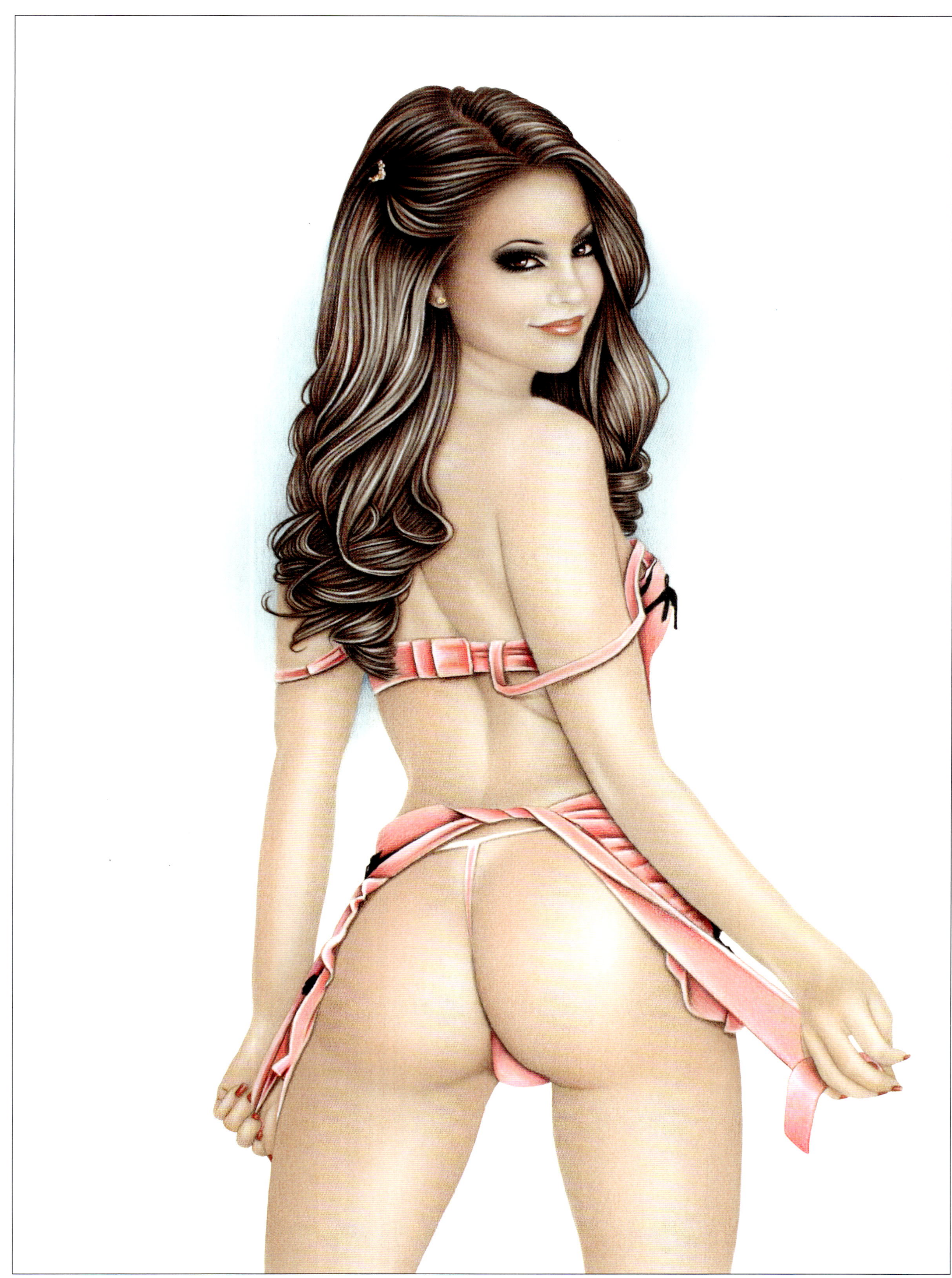

Culinary Delight